This Business of
PUBLISHING

An Insider's View of Current Trends and Tactics

Richard Curtis

ALLWORTH PRESS
NEW YORK

Published by Allworth Press
An imprint of Allworth Communications
10 East 23rd Street, New York NY 10010

Cover design by Douglas Design Associates, New York, NY

Page composition/typography by Sharp Des!gns, Inc., Lansing, MI

ISBN: 1-880559-98-6

Library of Congress Catalog Card Number: 98-70413

Printed in Canada

Contents

A review of the changes in publishing, for better or worse, since the author began writing about the publishing industry in the 1980s.

Section One: BIG PUBLISHING

The consignment system of selling books, making them returnable for credit, has destroyed publisher after publisher in the last fifty years, and threatens to continue doing so. With new electronic means of delivering information efficiently, the publishing industry must do something radical to end the hemorrhaging.

Why musical chairs in the publishing industry is ruining authors and orphaning books.

Section Two: UNDERSTANDING EDITORS

Section Three: PUBLISHING, TWENTY-FIRST-CENTURY STYLE

Section Four: UNDERSTANDING AUTHORS

Section Five: IS THERE A FUTURE?

Acknowledgments

MOST OF THE MATERIAL in this book originally saw the light of day in the pages of *Locus,* the fantasy and science-fiction magazine published by Charles Brown. I will always be indebted to him for turning the forum over to me for some twelve years.

Tad Crawford, my editor and the publisher of Allworth Press, was invaluable in organizing my disorderly collection of essays. For giving them a second life in book form, I thank him wholeheartedly.

All insights in this book have been field-tested on my wife, Leslie Tonner, who I consider to be the smartest publishing person I know, even though—or is it because?—she has never worked for a publishing company. And it is to her that this book is dedicated.

Preface: Then and Now

NEARLY TWO DECADES HAVE PASSED since I began writing about the publishing industry, and, as middle-aged people are wont to do, I recently browsed through my pile of tearsheets and wondered where the time had gone. Nostalgia is a sweet but essentially useless emotion, so, after dabbing the mist from my eyes, I took a harder look at the body of this work and began to ruminate on the changes that have occurred in the industry since 1981.

Our tradition-bound field evolves very slowly, but with the perspective of time, one can see definite trends—some good, some ominous. The advance of the publishing business toward monolithic consolidation continues inexorably, leaving almost no independent companies of large dimension operating today. The result is the emergence of a system for producing literature that might best be likened to dairy farming, with authors forced into the role of domesticated cattle resignedly allowing themselves to be milked to satisfy the thirst of a mass market. That the product will inevitably become homogenized goes without saying. Most distressing is the extension of these conditions to the book distribution system itself.

From my viewpoint, the most significant change in publishing in the last few years has been the tightening of the control exerted by bookstore chains over the creation of literature. Because purchasing decisions are made by a handful of buyers operating out of the chains' central headquarters, the leveraged influence of these buyers over decisions made by consumers, publishers, and, ultimately, writers has become immense. And because such decisions are usually reached by the calculation of the lowest common denominator, the selection process annually becomes more and more bestseller oriented. Aided by computerized sales information, the buyers tend to order in significant quantity only books by authors with proven track records, pushing publishers further and further into frontlist (just published), bottom-line, star-author, hit-book thinking, and putting increasing pressure on authors to truncate their apprenticeships, attempt to write blockbusters every time they sit down at their keyboards, and follow or repeat formulas. As this process evolves, our criteria for evaluating writers have begun to homogenize too, until we are left with only one: Is he or she a winner or a loser?

The winners become richer and the losers poorer. While star authors are now getting multimillion-dollar advances for their books, the starting pay for new authors and for writers working in genre fiction is pretty much what it was ten or fifteen years ago, somewhere between $1,500 and $5,000, and of course, if you adjust those figures for inflation, you will realize that struggling authors are horrendously worse off than they were in the 1960s and 1970s.

Although the rise of bookstore chains has improved the efficiency with which books are marketed to consumers, authors have not been the beneficiaries of profits created by that efficiency. For one thing, the returns problem has become colossal, meaning that while more copies of any given book may be getting into the stores, a higher percentage than ever before is being returned, and, of course, no royalty is paid on returned books. Higher return patterns also cause publishers to fix reserves against returns at higher figures, meaning lower and slower royalties.

For another thing, the bookstore chains, with their growing

stranglehold over publishers, are demanding and winning higher discounts, and because authors' royalty rates ride inversely on discount schedules, many authors are waking to discover disappointing, if not shocking, royalty statements even though their books shipped in large quantities. In fact, their royalty statements are disappointing *because* their books shipped in large quantities!

The level of interest in book discounting expressed by most authors is on a par with their interest in Manichaeism in fourth-century Persia. Although I can't blame them, it must be stated that their apathy is costing them dearly. Book publishing contracts provide for a reduction in royalty rate when the discount offered by the publisher to retail store or wholesale distributor exceeds a certain percentage. In some contracts the royalty is reduced by, say, half a point for every point by which the discount is increased. In others, the royalty is cut in half when the discount reaches a high level.

There is nothing inherently wrong with offering high discounts to induce buyers to order large quantities of merchandise. Nor is there anything wrong with tying authors' royalties to the discount rate. After all, the publisher is receiving less money for each unit sold, and it is only fair to ask the author to share in the reduced profit. Both publisher and author are compensated, however, by the high volume of sales. At least, both should be. In practice, however, authors lose out because most publishing contracts call for the same slashes in royalties today that existed ten or twenty years ago, before deep discounting became commonplace. For instance, your paperback royalty may, by contract, go from 8 percent to 4 percent if your publisher sells your book at a discount higher than 50 percent. In the 1970s, that discount was not given often; today, it is commonly exceeded. Yet, no one has told the authors, and even agents have been slow to realize the significance of the change. Late in 1985, three authors brought suit against Addison-Wesley, claiming that the publisher's interpretation of the discount clause had resulted in the loss of more than $100,000 in royalties. Although the authors were supposed to get a royalty of 15 percent of the list price per copy, the contract called for a drop in royalty to 10 percent of the publisher's net receipts for copies sold at half the list price or less. The publisher invoked that adjusted royalty on a large quantity of copies sold. The case was settled, but it underscored the necessity for authors and agents to recognize, and to build into contracts, the realities of modern book marketing.

Another disturbing development of the last half decade is the adoption by many publishers of an exceedingly restrictive option clause. Until the late 1970s, the option language in the boilerplate of most publishing contracts was fairly weak, giving the publisher little more than the right to see the author's next work before anybody else, and to negotiate in good faith for it. If publisher and author couldn't reach agreement, the author was free to seek a deal with another publisher.

This loose option made it easy for authors to leave their publishers, but with the stakes getting higher and higher, such freedom of movement became an alarming threat to publishers. Their legal counsels therefore started to build a more restrictive language into their option clauses, until today, the tight option is more the rule than the exception. (Paradoxically, the same language that enables a publisher to keep his sheep in the fold makes it harder for him to acquire sheep trying to leave that of his neighbors. He who lives by the option perishes by the option.)

Under the terms of the new option clauses, a publisher is granted a first look at the author's next work, as before, and the right to negotiate with the author. In the event negotiations break down, however, the publisher has the right to match the best offer that the author may secure from other publishers. Now, this is all well and good for the author who seeks only to get the very best price for his book. If, however, he is dissatisfied with his publisher and doesn't want to be published by that firm at any price, he's out of luck.

In my experience, an author's grounds for dissatisfaction are seldom restricted to money, and an author who is aggrieved with his publisher will not feel compensated by a raise in pay. The way options are designed today, however, the only legitimate way to escape from your publisher is to get a competitive house to make a bid for your book that is so high your original publisher can't match it. One cannot guarantee that will happen, however. Furthermore, the sophisticated language of some of the new options implies that you are in effect indentured to your publishers forever, as long as they continue matching the highest price you obtain in the marketplace. And, while I doubt that this interpretation would hold up in court, one publisher did recently attempt to invoke it to keep an author against her will. Only on threat of a lawsuit did the publisher decide, out of the goodness of his heart, to release the unhappy author. Agents like to boast that there isn't an option they cannot break, but the new phraseology is starting to spoil some perfect records.

Another significant change in contractual language has to do with electronic rights, specifically audio- and videotape cassettes. The last ten years have witnessed explosive growth in the consumption of videocassette recorders, Walkman-type tape players, and automobile audiotape cassette players, and the appetite for suitable programming has become ravenous. And now the Internet has opened unlimited markets for the exploitation of electronic rights.

Until recently, such rights were either reserved to authors as part of their motion picture and television rights, or, if they were granted to publishers, they were not exploited very aggressively because the market was so weak. Now, however, talking books, instructional tapes, and the like have become a source of intense contention between publishers and authors, and many publishers are quietly infiltrating contracts with language reserving those rights to themselves or granting themselves the right of first refusal to acquire those rights in the event that an outside company makes an offer for them to the author.

Not all the changes manifest in contracts over the last few years have been for the worse. At the time I started writing my column "Agent's Corner" in the 1980s, the only way that authors could secure insurance against the costs and judgments of libel and related lawsuits was to buy it themselves at exceedingly high premiums. Then a few publishers offered to include authors under the umbrella of their companies' libel insurance policies, free of charge. Many, but by no

Section One
Big Publishing

Last Chance

HE AMERICAN TRADE BOOK INDUSTRY is undergoing the most serious recession in its history, and though it has rebounded from other down cycles in the past, anyone who thinks it will return to boom times is living in a fool's paradise.

Trade book publishing has been in decline since the end of World War II. Industry boosters cite increased sales volume over that period to support the view that all is well, but much of the growth can be attributed to normal population increases and inflation. For the real story, one has but to look at the long roll call of publishers that have been forced to sell themselves to conglomerates, merge with larger publishing houses, or go out of business entirely. I am not speaking about mom-and-pop publishers operating on a shoestring; I'm referring to giants like Simon and Schuster, Doubleday, Bantam, Putnam, Macmillan, Scribner, Penguin, St. Martin's Press, and Harper and Row. Today, we are left with only seven or eight major trade book combines. Presumably, in this publisher-eat-publisher jungle, these survivors are the fittest. But are they any healthier than the weaklings they acquired?

Most of the resentment or suspicion that authors and agents feel toward publishers stems from royalty accounting based on returns. Authors, outraged that creative bookkeeping permits publishers to hold excessive royalties in the name of reserves against returns, consider the system fraudulent. Their viewpoint is easy to understand when you remember that returns are a manipulable form of currency. The temptation to manipulate them intensifies in recessionary or inflationary times when publishers seize upon royalty reserves as the most obvious source of cash to relieve their liquidity problems or earn some extra interest. Publishers cannot with impunity stop paying their printers, their landlords, their paper suppliers, or their employees. But by a stroke of the pen, raising the holdback on royalties from, say, 50 percent to 75 percent, a publisher can liberate enough cash to meet the urgent demands of all those other creditors—at the expense of authors. How, then, could authors, suffering liquidity problems of their own, not feel bitter? Nor is their mood improved to see their remaindered books, on which they receive little or no royalties, selling briskly in used-book stores.

Are there solutions to this dilemma? There are, but they all call for radical changes in the way we think about books, sell them, and account to each other for them. For any plan to succeed, it must: (1) allow publishers to print only as many copies as are necessary to fill orders, (2) put distribution on a nonreturnable basis, (3) enable publishers to make a profit, (4) encourage bookshops and chain stores to make money remaindering books on their own premises, and (5) provide authors with honest, easy-to-understand accounting. That's a tall order. Some gratifying attempts have been essayed, but they all failed because they were not radical enough, nor were they adopted on an industry-wide basis.

As a student of publishing history, I'm aware of all the "death-of-publishing" prophecies that have proven false in our time. But I don't think I'm risking much by stating that the publishing industry cannot endure much longer the way it is being run. The need to change our ways is particularly acute in light of revolutionary developments in electronic publishing.

In the coming era of "demand" publishing, we will see direct electronic delivery of text to reader-users without dependence on distributors, or even on paper. The technology for producing portable electronic books containing or accessing whole libraries is now at hand. By the start of the twenty-first century, thanks to computers, Nintendos, and Gameboys, a generation of children completely at ease with electronically delivered literature will make handheld electronic books the device of choice for reading. The awesome memory capacity of CDs, storing scores of volumes on miniature discs, may make bookstores and libraries obsolete. Thanks to the multimedia and interactive features of the new breed of computers, tomorrow's electronic books will entertain readers with audio and video displays that will make traditional books look as crude as cuneiform writing on stone tablets. Gone will be the disgustingly wasteful system of merchandising books, along with the creative bookkeeping that permits publishers to hold authors' money for years. Authors will be credited a royalty for each use of their property, and the purchase of books will be transacted by electronic debiting of consumers' charge accounts.

Until that day comes, we still have an industry to save. Toward the end of this book I will offer some possible options to reverse the downward spiral that has wreaked so much damage on our noble profession. If it is unworkable, I invite the industry to find one of its own. But find one it must, for at the rate we're going, it's only a matter of time before we read in these pages that the remaining behemoths of the publishing industry have succumbed to the same fate as all the others.

■

Orphans

THIS CHAPTER IS DEVOTED TO OR-
phans. I'm not referring to parentless children, but to books that have
no friends at the houses that publish them. Our hearts go out to
orphaned children. Our society seldom turns its back on them
completely. There are public and private institutions to support them,
foster and adoptive parents to nurture them. But for the abandoned
book there is no protective legislation, no foundling hospitals or
asylums, no big brothers, no champions or advocates. There are only
stunned authors, helpless agents, and publishers too caught up in the
hurly-burly of tomorrow's list to shed a tear for yesterday's.

Perhaps I'm getting nostalgic as I grow older, but I can't help
feeling that there have never been so many orphaned books as there
are today. If we can understand why, maybe we'll be able to do
something about them. The biggest cause is increased turnover of
editors. The most important friend a book has is the editor who
acquired it. Although publishing decisions at most houses today are
reached through a committee system, and production is nothing if not
a team effort, the sponsorship of a book generally remains with the

editor who first read it, recommended and defended it at editorial board meetings, negotiated the contract for it, shepherded it through production, and presented it to the sales staff. Because enthusiasm is the most important attitude in the publishing process, as long as that editor remains in place, you can expect a certain measure of commitment to see a book through, to ignite company enthusiasm, talk the book up to the trade, push the salespeople—and, if nothing else, make the author feel that someone is watching over his or her baby.

Unfortunately, editors don't stay still long enough these days to see books through. They quit, or are fired, or are squeezed out of merged or acquired companies, leaving behind whole lists of books in one critical stage of development or another. I have no statistics to prove that editorial tenure is shorter these days than it used to be, and certainly I have none to prove that the best publishers seem to be those with the most staff longevity and stability. I only know from bitter experience that whenever an editor leaves a company, an author is going to end up paying for it.

Very few books emerge unharmed by the departure of their sponsoring editors. Big books may, because their importance and value are sufficient to ensure that in-house enthusiasm will not be fatally injured and company ranks will close the gap. But even big books will be hurt if an editor in chief or other high-ranking executive leaves, creating a decision vacuum that affects all titles great and small.

The departure of an editor is a traumatic event in the life of a book, if not that of the author. An editor's commitment is the fuel that propels a book through the shoals threatening it from every point of the compass. Not the least of these, by the way, is the hostility of other editors in the publishing company.

Publishers are no different from most other types of business when it comes to office politics, and editors compete hotly with each other for more attention for their own books, frequently at the expense of rival editors' books. It's easy to see, then, why an editor's departure can absolutely shatter the relationship of the book and author to the publisher, leaving books prey to countless vicissitudes.

Sometimes continuity is achieved by the departed editor's replacement. But all too often the replacement has his or her own list to worry about, or is more intent on acquiring new books than on attending to someone else's legacies. The result: another harvest of orphans. I know of one author who ruefully boasts that by the publication date of each of his eight books, the editors who had acquired them were no longer with the company.

Bumper crops of orphans are yielded after the acquisition of one publisher by another and after the merger of two houses. The havoc takes many forms. Hardest hit, of course, are books and book projects in development or prepublication production at the acquired company. Naturally, the new owners must reevaluate that list to determine whether the books fit in with their editorial programs. For editors and executives already burdened by their own ongoing workloads, this review process cannot be accomplished overnight. Big books and a few others in critical stages may get emergency attention, but the rest are put in a state of suspended animation while their fates are being considered. The staff of the acquired company may be retained for a while to see the current list through, but the loss of momentum is still, all too often, crippling.

Backlist books of the acquired company also, too frequently, get short shrift. Harder to demonstrate is the damage done to the past and present lists of the acquiring company, but there can be little question that continuity is interrupted, decisions delayed, enthusiasms hobbled.

As I write this, paperback publishing is only regaining its feet after still another turbulent year. The number of books affected by these changes was hundreds, if not thousands, depending on how serious you feel the effects were. In some cases, scarcely a beat was missed as the guard was changed; in others, whole lines, lists, and series were canceled or put on hold. As rumors about other companies in trouble or up for sale continue, it's entirely possible we haven't seen the end of a revolution that has left an army of shell-shocked authors.

The forces affecting the fates of books are not always as convulsive as acquisitions, mergers, bankruptcies, or wholesale job-hopping. Lesser and quieter events can also have discouraging effects on the spirits of editorial staffs, causing them to turn their backs on books they had so lovingly acquired. Modest advance sales, a few negative early reviews, news of a competing book, all can take the wind out of an editor's or salesperson's sails; doubts arise, enthusiasm wanes, momentum is checked.

These reactions are translatable into dollars: How much more should we spend on the book? Will a greater financial commitment put the book over the top, or will it be a case of throwing good money after bad?

Unfortunately, in this age of growing bureaucratization in the publishing business, as the adventurous entrepreneur publisher gives way to cautious editorial committees subservient to corporate business administrators, conservatism and negativism have become the prevailing attitudes when such decisions have to be made. This means, in turn, that if money is going to be invested in any book, it will be invested in the sure thing, the latest book by a big-name author with a successful track record.

This, in turn, creates still more orphaned books, for, with publishing firms committing most of their resources only to guaranteed bestsellers, the amount of money available for more marginal and midlist books is diminished. Thankfully, there has been a countertrend in the rise of imaginative, aggressive small presses capable of exploiting types of books that major houses are afraid, or can't afford, to do. But many agents are unsure which of these presses are solidly funded and which are underfinanced, so they tend to be cautious in their dealings with them. ("I don't do business with publishers I can't reach by taxi," one of my colleagues sniffs.) Another hopeful sign is that some major publishers are creating "boutique" imprints that combine the intimate attention to authors associated with small presses with the mighty distribution capabilities of the parent companies. But I'm skeptical that these developments will reverse the fundamental trend.

Is there anything authors can do to prevent their books from being heartlessly turned out into the cold? To a degree there is. Some preventive measures, for instance, may be taken at the contractual negotiation stage. You may be able to sharpen the language of the assignment provisions of your contract prohibiting the publisher from assigning your contract to another firm without your express permission. Thus, in a corporate takeover, you might be able to withdraw your book if you felt it was going to be lost in the shuffle, and peddle it elsewhere. You might structure your option clause to become null and void if the firm is sold or merged, so that even if there is nothing you can do about the present book, you are not obligated to offer your next one to the same company. There is also the stipulation commonly known as the "editor's clause," meaning that if your editor moves to another publisher, you have the option of moving your book with him or her.

Many conscientious editors, when changing jobs, do try to bring along with them some or all of their list, for they know what fate is in store for the books left behind. But much depends on the extent to which the old publisher is willing to part with the books, and how much the new one wants them brought over. If the option to leave them where they are or to send them to a new home belongs to the author, perhaps the book will have a fighting chance.

Why doesn't every contract have an editor's clause? One reason is that publishers don't like them very much, for such provisions make it easy for a valued editor, to leave a firm. Another reason is the diminution of attachment between authors and editors. With all the musical chairs being played in the editorial job market, few editors stick around long enough for such strong ties to develop. So authors don't ask for editor's clauses in their contracts, knowing that so many editors are here today, gone tomorrow. Still, an editor's clause would furnish some degree of comfort and flexibility for many authors, and they should try to work one into their contracts at the time of negotiation.

Supposing you don't have these contractual defenses to call on, or are unwilling or unable to exercise them (because, say, your book is already printed and it's too late to pull it out), there are, nevertheless, tactics available to you to try to rescue your book from oblivion.

If your editor has left the company (or the company has left your editor) and your book is still at a fairly early stage, when an editor's involvement can make a difference, then you or your agent should contact the new editor and reintroduce the book and its author. Even though the new editor may already have been briefed about it, your personal contact may enable him to form an attachment to it that could make a difference when the book is entering the rapids of publication. If the book is beyond the stage where an editor can help, you can try to go higher, to the head of the company, to petition him to familiarize himself with the book, get excited about it, push the salespeople, spend a little money on ads or promotion. You might introduce yourself to a few key people at your company—the sales manager, marketing director, head of advertising and publicity—and point out some ways they can boost the book.

Obviously, you may have to take matters into your own hands. You may, for instance, create your own promotional tours, buy ad space, and otherwise publicize your books. This calls for no small degree of determination, nerve and money, but rescue missions have always done so. Sadly and ironically, publishers don't always appreciate an author's independent activities on behalf of his or her book, and a few have been downright obstructionist. Recently, for example, an author I know decided to undertake her own campaign for a book for which the publisher had done nothing, a book that looked, in the author's words, "as if it was about to be dropped down the tube." She visited every bookstore in her city's phone book, romancing the owners and hyping her book. What did she get for it? A phone call from her publisher saying, "We wish you wouldn't do that—we get into trouble when an author promotes a book and then people can't find it in the stores."

The tragedy of an orphaned book can in no way be compared to that of an orphaned child, except perhaps for the amount of time it takes to bring both into the world. Yet, for those of us who have invested our love in writing a book, agenting it, acquiring or editing or manufacturing it, surely there must be more to be done than presiding over its remaindering with a shrug. Someone loved that book once; someone thought other people would love it too. That's why it was written, bought, and published.

Can't we try harder to save the orphans?

■

Wholesaler Revolution

A QUIET BUT NASTY RESTRUCTUR-
ing of the wholesale paperback distribution business in the mid-1990s
played a major role in accelerating the destruction of two already
endangered species: midlist and category fiction. It can be argued, in
fact, that the shock waves of this event triggered some major upheavals in the publishing industry a year later, ranging from top-level
editorial turnovers to the cancellation of books—indeed, in one case,
cancellation of an entire list of books.

Generally speaking, there are two ways paperback books are
distributed: direct and wholesale. Publishers that ship their books to
bookstores or bookstore chains are said to be selling direct. But in
order to sell their books to supermarkets, drug and candy stores, and
specialty shops, it is easier for them to use distribution agencies that
stock racks in their territories with books, as well as magazines and
other products. Though the agencies charge a commission, they
perform a service that publishers couldn't possibly undertake themselves, and they often reach a far wider audience than bookstores can
ever hope to. Until the collapse of this system in the mid-nineties, these

companies engaged commissioned, independent individuals to service the vast and sprawling marketplace in the heartland of America.

The traditional model of an independent paperback distributor is a sole practitioner going from account to account in a station wagon filled with paperbacks and magazines, stocking the racks according to his own judgment, past experience, and intimate knowledge of the taste and eccentricities of the accounts along his route. His decisions were subject to many influences and pressures not always relevant to the quality of the books he handled. Thus, many authors promoting their books visited these independent operators in the hope of influencing them into stocking extra copies of their books on the racks along their routes. Many a romance author brought coffee and donuts out to an independent distributor in the cold predawn hours as he stocked his station wagon, then pitched her book to him, charmed him into adding a few extra copies to the racks along his route, and posed with him for a photograph on his tailgate.

By the early eighties, this idyllic image had begun to clash with the realities of computer-based book ordering as developed by chain bookstores. Why, these agencies asked, do we have to use this clunky and costly system when we can order directly from publishers using computer-generated shopping lists? Instead of hundreds of titles distributed by hundreds of independent men and women operating on hunches, friendships, and other hard-to-calculate criteria, why don't we just buy prepacks of the top sellers and stock all the stores in our territory with them? Give me three Grishams, three Stephen Kings, two Danielle Steels, one Clive Cussler, etc.

This new approach was elementarily simple: it required but a few decisions by a handful of executives—decisions often based on the author's computerized sales history rather than on the value of the books themselves. If increased efficiency and maximum profit was the goal, the strategy succeeded brilliantly. But the cost? According to Tom Doherty, publisher of Tor and Forge paperbacks, after one super-market chain solicited bids to stock paperback racks throughout its stores, the losing independents sold out to the winner, plunging the number of operators from 111 to 7! In a Texas territory, 21 independent agencies were similarly boiled down to 4 almost overnight.

The toll on authorship was also catastrophic if not harder to quantify, but the driving out of competition caused the number of available paperback "pockets" or "slots" to shrink. The effects filtered down as publishers demanded more and more books of mainstream size and feel, rather than formula fiction in genres such as romance, westerns, thrillers, and science fiction. Literary agents thus found it harder to place new authors, even in those hitherto invulnerable categories, and came under increasing pressure to deliver blockbusters. The ripples rocked many hardcover houses as editors were forced to become choosier about buying books that didn't have big paperback reprint potential.

The waves reached tsunami proportion when HarperCollins canceled over one hundred titles in an effort to cut costs. The grounds were either that the books did not promise to make a profit in the current market or that the authors had missed their contractual deadlines and were therefore in default of their contracts. Though the authors were paid off the balances of their advances, the axing was brutal and with little precedent, and it brought home to everyone that the publishing industry had gone from a "profession for gentlemen" to a profession for marketing directors and certified public accounts. It is hard to fault publishers for trying to survive, but with returns averaging 30–50 percent for most trade books, they had little choice but to go after the tried-and-true stars and formulas in the hope that that would increase the "sell-through" percentage of copies distributed.

Even before this turmoil, many nonbookstore outlets such as supermarkets and drugstores had begun to wonder whether books were worth the cost of carrying them, and to replace racks carrying comparatively low-margin paperbacks with displays of faster-moving and more profitable merchandise. Or they reduced their rack space to accommodate only the top ten or fifteen bestselling authors. As one supermarket executive told me, "If it's a choice of paperbacks or pantyhose, I'll carry whichever product moves faster. Culture is fine, but it still has to earn me a profit."

A paperback sales manager I spoke to reckoned that some 160,000 rack pockets were lost to pantyhose and other products in a two-year period as a result of these market forces. Some of the slack has been picked up by expanding superstore book chains with their enormous leverage of purchasing and discounting power. But the chains' emphasis on bestsellers only adds to the blockbuster mentality. The dramatic rise in paper costs in recent years has also forced publishers to drop the types of books that no longer generate big profits. The attraction of other media such as movies, television, the Internet, and computer games may also be siphoning off readers or adding to an orientation that sees books strictly as works of mass entertainment rather than vehicles of ideas and culture.

Computerized ordering may be a more professional way of distributing books, and it might well cut down the terrible returns numbers that have made the wholesale business such a nightmare. But it also adds to the loss of vital personal contact along the chain of author to distributor to store owner to consumer. Some independents have gone to work for their conquerors, but even if there are jobs available, many who characterize themselves as entrepreneurs and individualists find it too hard to become mere truck drivers with no discretion over what they carry or how they distribute it.

Although some of the emerging super-wholesalers are more category oriented, offer a wide variety of books, and carry an inventory of backlist favorites, the pressure to boil the list down to its lowest common denominator is intense. The phenomenon is particularly visible in stores and kiosks at airports.

The process also forces authors to imitate bestseller formulas and second-guess what the mass consumer wants to read, making for further homogenization and mediocrity and fueling reader flight from books to media that are perceived as more interesting or entertaining. Geoff Hannell, former Publisher of Harper Paperbacks and now an executive with Dove Books, told me that the turbulent forces in the wholesale business would definitely increase efficiency and lower returns percentages, but he also conceded that, "there seems to be less risk taking now in terms of product." One head of a paperback company predicted that in two years all decisions about the wholesale distribution of paperbacks will be entirely in the hands of no more than ten people. If those kingpins succumb to the temptation to take the easy way of prepackaging the latest hits by brand-name authors and abandoning lower-margin but more intellectually stimulating books, the decline of consumer choice will accelerate yet again.

Book readers really yearn for choice, and the advent of online bookstores such as Amazon.com proves it. The company has designed a Web site offering consumers immense amounts of information about tens of thousands of books, the majority of which are not immediately available but can be located through electronic search of the inventories of bookstores and wholesale warehouses. Purchases are securely charged against the user's credit card and delivered promptly unless the book in question is hard to find.

The wholesaler revolution is not going to stop with Amazon.com and its flood of imitators. The next step, publishing on demand, will enable the book consumer to sit down in a bookstore kiosk, insert his credit card, order any book of his choice, and in minutes download a bound copy, printed from text stored in a vast memory bank. If this seems visionary, it is in fact already happening, especially in the college market where it is cheaper for students to acquire texts through "custom publishing" than to buy them in traditional form in traditional stores.

Revolutions have a way of consuming themselves in their own flames, and one can visualize a day when consumers order books directly from publishers if not authors. The concept is called "disintermediation," or going around the intermediate. Why should I physically visit a bookstore to download a book, when I can do the same at home? The answer—for now—is that it's inconvenient to read a book in the form of a pile of downloaded, hard-copy pages, and besides, I don't have the machinery to bind it. But that's not what's going to happen. What's going to happen is that I will load the text into a handheld reading device that "plays" it on a screen that looks and feels like a traditional paper book. The wholesaler revolution will be complete—because there won't be any more wholesalers!

■

Big

I'VE FREQUENTLY SAID THAT IN THIS turbulent world of publishing, with its tectonic upheavals and head-spinning personnel changes, the only oases of stability are the literary agencies. "We were here yesterday, we're here today, and we'll be here tomorrow," we like to reassure our clients. But some recent developments have authors, editors, and agents wondering whether destabilization is about to rock the agencies as well.

The merger in the mid-eighties of Sterling Lord's agency with a firm of more recent vintage, Peter Matson's Literistics, was the first of these events. Then, the end of 1988 saw the reorganization of Curtis Brown Ltd.'s New York and London offices and the mega-merger of former ICM superstar agent Lynn Nesbit with Mort Jankow's block-buster shop. Are these the precursors of a merger spree among literary agencies? Will rich and powerful agents start gobbling up smaller ones after the pattern of publishers, advertising agencies, and banks? Should the clients of small, independent agencies be concerned about their agents' abilities to compete with the biggies? Are we tumbling toward a world in which the surviving two or three publishers are serviced by the surviving two or three literary agencies?

Some observers say yes, claiming that in order to deal with a conglomeratized and internationalized publishing industry, the agents must follow suit. In each of the three cases mentioned above, spokespeople stated that their blended agencies would be in a better position to cope with the emerging multinational publishing giants. How accurate are their assessments?

There can be no question that the tentacles of the major publishing companies are extending overseas. In the last few years, global mergers and acquisitions have come to a boil. Harper, St. Martin's, Putnam, Holt, and Bantam Doubleday Dell are among the great publishers that are now run by overseas bosses. At the same time, American-owned publishers like Random House and Simon & Schuster have bought into foreign companies in the last few years.

These transactions point to a future inevitably dominated by multinational superpublishers. Authors and agents can now look forward to increased pressure from American publishers to license world rights in all languages, so that the primary houses can feed books to their overseas subsidiaries and keep everything in the family. Is this necessarily a bad thing? Not if the foreign sister-houses do a good job and there is no loss of income to authors.

However, because world rights deals preclude competitive bidding for a book in any given foreign country, there is a genuine danger that authors will *not* realize top dollar—or pound, mark, franc, or yen—for their work in overseas markets. Equally discomfiting is the possibility that some of the foreign publishers to which American books are fed will be inappropriate for those books. American authors and agents may want to fight to reserve foreign rights and to select their own foreign publishers, choosing those that offer the most money or the most comfortable editorial environment. But if we are left with only eight or nine major consortia to sell books to, our freedom of choice will almost certainly be strangled.

Statements made by the recently merged or reorganized literary agencies express hope that they will be in a stronger position to uphold that freedom of choice. In announcing the marriage of Sterling Lord and Literistics, a stronger presence in England and other overseas territories was cited as a key motive for the union. Curtis Brown's announcement of restructuring of its London and New York offices projected "a closely interlocked global literary agency with active offices in New York, London, Toronto, and Sydney." The merger was designed to enable Curtis Brown's clients "to better meet the challenge presented by the vast international mergers of publishers," according to *Publishers Weekly*. *PW's* coverage of the Nesbit-Janklow partnership noted "a reaction to the internationalization and consolidation among publishers" as one important reason for this merger. Not a few authors and agents reading about these developments are wondering if the wave of the future is for literary agents to form or join immense combines of their own in order to deal effectively with these behemoth publishers. But is this necessarily so?

As currently constituted, the literary agency field is populated by hundreds of companies ranging in size from sole practitioner to firms employing numerous agents and handling hundreds of authors. This number has not shrunk since I entered the profession, and indeed seems to have expanded as big money opportunities attracted newcomers. The oft-stated remark among agents that there is enough business for all of us remains true as far as I have been able to observe. Most of these agents make good livings, and though we all worry about the dangers posed by publishing mergers and internationalizations, few that I have spoken to feel a compelling need to sacrifice their hard-won independence to some conglomerate of agencies in order to maintain their competitive edge.

Why? Because agents understand clearly that their power and influence do not derive merely from the number of clients they represent but from the quality of those clients. Naturally, an agency with twenty big-name authors will have more clout than one with just two or three. But does that mean the new kid on the block, the agent just going into business, can't get a foot in the door? The answer is: If his client list contains some attractive moneymakers, he will get the same respectful audience with a publisher that any other agent does.

If new agents are at a disadvantage, it's the same one suffered by tyros in any other field of endeavor. All it takes for an agent to find the doors of the publishing business flung wide open for him is one hit author or even one hit book. "It's not how big you are," literary agent Georges Borchardt remarked to me, "It's what you have to sell." And if what you have to sell is a superstar author, you can just about write your own contract.

One agent, responding to news of the Nesbit-Jankow partnership, speculated that their association, "with its formidable clout, could, if it desired, change some industry customs that authors find objectionable, such as option clauses in contracts." I am skeptical that any individual agency is capable of wielding that much influence. Certain publishing policies are so deeply rooted throughout the industry that although a powerful agent can bend them for his own clients, he cannot get them altered for the benefit of all authors. Abuses of option clauses, bad-faith interpretations of the acceptability provision of contracts, and untruth in royalty reporting will not yield to anything less than collective action waged by organizations of authors or agents. Whenever such action has been undertaken, it has produced important achievements. Recently, a team of agents from the Association of Authors' Representatives took a publisher to lunch to review some of his company's policies. "Gee, I don't think I've ever been taken to lunch by an agent," the publisher said. "You're being taken to lunch by three hundred agents," one of the delegates pointedly reminded him.

The notion that superagencies would have greater leverage in the international marketplace merits particular analysis, for it suggests that a literary agent must have branches or subagencies throughout the world in order to be competitive. There are several ways for agents to license British and translation rights to their clients' work. The first is exquisitely simple: throw them into the American deal. In other words, sell worldwide publication rights to the U.S. publisher and let that publisher worry about them. By doing so, the publisher becomes the agent or co-agent for British and translation rights, taking a commission on them as any other agent would do.

This may seem like the lazy way out. It is certainly an expensive one, as most publishers charge commissions upwards of 25 percent exclusive of subagents' commissions. If your U.S. publisher takes 25 percent foreign commission and your contract does not require your publisher to take care of subagents' 10 percent commission, the total commission on that foreign deal will be 35 percent, not 25 percent. The author's share will be applied towards the unearned U.S. advance, and if the unearned balance is large enough, he may never see any part of that foreign money at all. If he does, and his agent takes a commission on it, his net share is reduced even further. The advance that an American publisher pays for world rights would have to be large enough to compensate the author for all that he would have made if he or his agent reserved foreign rights and sold them to the same publishers. Most agents, to my knowledge, charge no more than 20 percent for foreign rights, take care of subagents out of that commission, and, of course, do not apply authors' net proceeds toward an unearned advance.

Nevertheless, any agent *can* become a worldwide player by simply selling British and translation rights to American publishers. Most agents prefer to try reserving those rights, for the economic reasons I've described. They then have a number of options for disposing of them. They can sell them directly to foreign publishers, they can sell them through foreign subagents and split commissions with them, or they can sell them through wholly-owned subsidiaries placed in overseas territories.

If an author reserves foreign rights, the author and agent are better able to pick the best foreign publishers for the book, get the highest prices, and select compatible editors. Peter Ginsberg, an agent with Curtis Brown, felt that the restructuring of his agency would enable Curtis Brown agents in key English language territories (the United States, Great Britain, Canada, and Australia) to coordinate and fine-tune the packaging of international deals to an extraordinary degree. But he certainly didn't rule out the traditional approach employed by smaller agencies. "There will always be excellent opportunities for small, independent agents," he told me, "but today's agents must be much more aware of the international situation when they structure deals than they used to be." An independent agent with splendid subagents or even no subagents at all can move just as forcefully as any worldwide agency if the property is hot enough and the agent is smart enough. Bear in mind that a great part of international literary traffic is category and midlist material, requiring a more routine approach to foreign licensing. It isn't likely that a multinational mega-agency will be able to flog a traditional cowboy novel or romance much better than any other agency.

Unfortunately, those types of books seldom make headlines, so we are left with the impression that the agency business is going global. It isn't. The motives behind the cluster of agency mergers are highly complex and individual and don't signify the start of any trend. Authors shouldn't worry about it. They have much bigger things to worry about, such as the integrity of their creative spirit. This point was cogently made in a recent think-piece in *Publishers Weekly* by Herbert M. Katz, a former publisher turned literary agent. "Is the development of a writer best served by membership in a killer literary organization?" he asked." Do I want my writers to measure their happiness by the size of their paychecks, the way everyone else seems to—or do I want them to feel that even now, there is something special about the choice of writing as a job?" For Katz, as for most of the literary agents I know, "the greatest defense an author can have against an industry now gone to bigness is the kind of representation that is not going to encourage the writer to engage in the publisher's box-office thinking."

Bigness is certainly one viable way for agents to respond to the monolithic formations of today's publishers. But expansion, acquisition, and internationalization for their own sakes are not going to solve anything for agents any more than they have for publishers. The greatest challenge of modern publishing is to preserve the human values that drive the creative spirit of both writers and publishing people. Standing as they do between these two worlds, literary agents are uniquely positioned to carry out this mandate. It is vitally important for us not to let bigness or smallness obscure the issue.

■

Incentives? Or Schmears?

BISMARCK SAID THAT IT IS UNWISE to look too closely into the way we make our laws or our sausages. You may be able think of some other things that don't bear up too well under intense scrutiny. High on my list is what publishers, particularly mass-market paperback publishers, have to do these days to get their merchandise displayed in and promoted by bookstores. It might be described as publishing's dirty little secret, except that it's not so little. In fact, it's become so pervasive that it touches everybody in publishing, even though not everybody is aware of it yet.

In fact, not everybody wants to know about it. A friend of mine, a top-notch paperback salesman, phoned me a while back to tell me he had just been hired by a hardcover publisher to launch its mass-market paperback line. "That's great," I said. "In eight weeks you'll be back on the street looking for another job."

"What do you mean?" he gasped.

"I don't think your boss wants to know what you have to do to get paperbacks sold. When he finds out, he'll want no part of it."

He reflected for a moment, "Yeah, well, it *does* get kind of nasty out there. And this man's such a gentleman . . ."

"That's why I give it eight weeks."

In due time he phoned me again, "You were wrong. It wasn't eight weeks. It was seven."

One of the things my friend's former boss didn't want to know about is exemplified by a good news–bad news story told to me by another publisher, the head of a small hardcover house. It happens that he was about to publish a celebrity biography and was pitching it at a bookstore chain. "We love it," the buyer said to him. "In fact, we'd like to do a feature piece about it in our promotional catalog."

"Wonderful!" said the publisher.

"It will cost you $7,500," the buyer said to him.

The publisher reeled with shock—but he ended up paying the $7,500. Why? "The alternative," he said, "was worse,"—meaning that had he not paid it, he was afraid that the chain would not carry the book.

This good news–bad news story is anything but a joke, for such experiences are common among publishers today. With far more books published than there is bookstore space to accommodate them comfortably, the struggle for advantage has driven publishers to resort to desperate and sometimes dubious measures. Just how dubious they are may be inferred by the number of publishing people who refuse to talk on the record about them. Although none stated that these measures are corrupt, neither could any deny that there is a bad aroma in the air around the book retailing business.

Paperback publishers and chains are locked in a serious predicament. Most publishers readily admit that there are too many books published. But none of them is willing to cut back on hard-won rack space. Rather than sacrifice that space, they fill it monthly with midlist genre titles, unnecessary reissues, and "nonbooks" that many bookstores feel they could easily live without. If publishers ever gave up that space, voluntarily or otherwise, they would lose a slot they might urgently want back one day to fill with a major release.

The problem is particularly acute in the nonbookstore chains, such as merchandise and food marts, where bookracks compete for space with breakfast cereal, toilet paper, or automobile products. There, an average of 128 slots are allotted for some 450 titles issued monthly. With four books funneling into the space available for only one, something has to give: either fewer books will be displayed, or books will be displayed for less than a month so that all titles can get some time (one week) in the sun. In most nonbookstore outlets, the latter solution is impractical, and so books remain on display for one month. But which books? How are the 128 finalists per month selected (fewer, actually, because so-called superreleases often take up more than one slot)? Well, as buyers for those stores are not particularly sophisticated about books, it should not be surprising that they often respond to the publisher offering them the most alluring inducements to stock a title.

The larger bookstores and bookstore chains do have more space to accommodate the monthly flood of books, perhaps not all 450 but certainly a good deal more than 128. For these retailers, then, the problem is not space but rather time and attention. A publisher wants to see its books carried in a store for eight weeks, and displayed in the front where they catch the attention of browsers. Unless some kind of deal is proffered to the store, however, the unfit titles will survive on the shelf for a week instead of a month or two, particularly if they are not bylined by star authors. Books by stars usually get all the time and space they need; they sell themselves without a major investment of time and energy on the part of bookstore personnel. It's on the level of secondary books that the war is fought.

To overcome the problems of inadequate display space or inadequate display time for those books, publishers have developed the means to equalize the survival rate. One technique is to pay wholesalers a "slotting allowance" to carry certain titles on their shelves, to display them more prominently, or to promote them as bestsellers.

Another technique is to offer stores incentives in the form of extra discounts as a reward for meeting certain purchase quotas. These discount schedules are issued to all stores and are supposed to be applicable to all without favoritism. However, when deciding between an independent bookstore or small chain that can buy a small number of copies of a given title, and a giant chain that has the capacity to purchase many thousands, it is understandably hard for a publisher to refrain from offering a little something extra to the big buyer. Such discriminatory practices were asserted to be in restraint of trade in a legal action brought against several major paperback book companies by the Northern California Booksellers Association in the mid-eighties. Although the suit was settled, and the publishers have modified their discount schedules to make them equally accessible to all bookstores, the pressures that created the discriminatory practices haven't changed one bit, and revised discount policies may still be favoring the larger store chains. And the offering or soliciting of secret discounts is by no means unheard of, according to some sources I interviewed.

Another area where ethical distinctions become blurry is the bookstore catalogue. In order to push their merchandise, independent bookstores or store chains issue a variety of promotional literature to the trade and to consumers. Obviously, not all the titles described in that literature will be afforded equal treatment: the ones that the publishers or stores are hyping will get featured coverage. Such coverage is expensive, however, and the stores cannot be expected to bear the load unsubsidized.

Most publishers do not begrudge stores a reasonable contribution to the production costs of catalogues. But some feel that the charges go beyond reasonable. It is impossible to determine whether or not this is so. For example, one recent bookstore chain rate card, issued to publishers in connection with its Preferred Reader Program—a sort of book club offering discounts and other benefits to members—invited publisher participants to pay $50,000 for a "top tier" in the Preferred Reader guide that the chain was to send out before Christmas. For that sum, a title would be one of ten books featured on a page in the Guide, get front-of-store display, and receive featured treatment in radio and newspaper ads. Was it worth $50,000 or more in sales to the publisher? If not, the publisher was free to elect a lower tier in the chain's program. On the fifth tier, for instance, $6,500 paid for a title to be one of fifteen on a page in the holiday catalogue but nothing more. Indeed, a publisher could elect not to feature a title in the catalogue at all—and risk being frozen out of all but the diminishing number of independent bookstores.

This very viewpoint was expressed to me by a publisher, who said, "The principal intent of these charges is not to sell books, it's to make a profit for the chains. Better than 50 percent of the time, advertising in a chain catalogue is not the way a publisher would spend his money if he had a choice. But we don't have a choice, and that's where we cross the line between voluntary co-op advertising and . . . well, maybe you can think of a polite way of putting it."

Although the large bookstore chains may not be all-powerful, it is nevertheless extremely intimidating to challenge them, and if you try, you'd better have some heavy artillery. One executive of a hardcover house told me about an experience he had when trying to line up a featured Christmas catalogue position for a forthcoming book by a major bestselling writer. "They told us it would cost $26,000, and we told them to go to hell. They implied that they might not carry the book. We said fine, their competitor across the street will carry it. When they realized that they needed us as much as we needed them, they proposed a compromise. Some compromise! We took a smaller, cheaper ad in the catalogue. But it did save face all around. I don't think we would have been so daring if the book hadn't been so important."

Chain-store people feel that the catalogue issue is misunderstood, and they claim that they are actually doing publishers a favor by channeling money into catalogue displays. They reason as follows: trade publishers contribute co-op advertising money to bookstore chains. They declare their co-op policies in writing. This money may either be applied to the cost of book ads in newspapers, or to *anything else that will have the equivalent effect of an ad.* And some chains feel that a feature in their catalogue, which is distributed to many thousands of accounts, is as effective as a couple of $10,000 or $20,000 ads in the *New York Times,* and maybe more. And even when stores or store chains do agree to take out a co-op book ad in a magazine or newspaper, the benefit often inures more to the publisher than to the sponsoring store, for consumers are attracted to the book in that ad, not necessarily to the store. Furthermore, print advertising space is usually cheaper for retailers than it is for publishers. By laying out the cost of the co-op ads, the stores confer a tremendous savings upon the publishers—a savings that publishers ill reward by settling their co-op bills very slowly, according to one store executive.

Another, and equally disturbing, practice requires publishers to pay bookstore chains a fee for the use of shelf space. It was originally developed by food and other merchandise chains. New manufacturers, or manufacturers attempting to distribute new lines and products, are charged what might be called an entry fee by the chain stores in order to guarantee that those stores will stock and display the merchandise. Although book distribution, particularly paperback book distribution, has never been one of the more savory branches of the publishing business (it's an offshoot of the trucking industry), the application of food-store chain "slotting allowances" to books today has been made possible by the rise of the enormous wholesale and retail bookstore chains in the last few decades.

Before we hasten to judgment, I should state that I was told that this concept was introduced not by the chains but by publishing executives seeking a competitive edge, and much of the initiative continues to come from publishers. ("How the hell do you think my books get on the shelves—jump up there by themselves?" one publisher growled at me.) But even if publishers do take the lead, the chains do not exactly mount vicious resistance. What is more likely is that publishers and booksellers are now locked in a nasty cycle of mutual inducement (there: I did find a polite way of putting it). It's a cycle from which no one is sure he wants to be released. "It's a terrible situation," one independent bookseller joked, "How come we're not taking advantage of it?"

In any event, today, slotting allowances are accepted as a necessity of doing business. New publishers, or publishers starting new lines and imprints, are confronted with the necessity of paying for the privilege of having their merchandise attractively positioned, or positioned at all. Publishers are often charged for dumps and other displays and for front-of-store positioning.

A typical example is a "Wholesaler Incentive Plan" offered by one paperback publisher. Among a variety of inducements offered in this letter to wholesale accounts is a schedule of payments to be made for positioning certain titles on the stores' bestseller list:

- 25¢ per copy to assist you in promoting the book slotted in your top 1 through 5
- 15¢ per copy to assist you in promoting the book slotting in your top 6 through 10
- 10¢ per copy to assist you in promoting the book slotted in your top 11 through 15
- 5¢ per copy to assist you in promoting the book slotted in your top 16 through 20

The books thus promoted actually go on a bestseller list: not the *Publishers Weekly* or *New York Times* bestseller list, but a distributor's bestseller list, similar to a food chain's weekly features. Store customers will thus see racks of "bestsellers" that do not necessarily have anything to do with nationwide lists. But the positions on those lists have been paid for with cash, and from the publishers' and stores' viewpoints, a bestseller is a bestseller.

Chain store and wholesaler spokespersons do not consider any of this unusual or alarming. They take the position that if a publisher thinks its book is terrific, let that publisher back up its claim with hard cash. One publisher did just that, and was therefore able to elevate a midlist author into a bestselling one. "As brutal as the system may be," he says, "in his case it worked. Ask that author if *he* thinks the system is unethical!" This may be a shortsighted attitude, however, because it does not take into account the financial and other tolls that fall upon publishers, consumers, and, ultimately, writers.

The dangers inherent in the practices I have described compelled the late Roberta Grossman, then publisher of Zebra/Pinnacle Books, to speak out in an article in *Magazine and Bookseller,* a publishing industry trade publication. This is the only instance I know of when a publishing person has gone on record on these matters, and if an executive of Zebra, a company that is no slouch in the aggressive marketing of its books, speaks out in concern, there is a great deal for the rest of us to be concerned about, too:

> Every time a publisher buys a book, he is putting his money where his mouth is in terms of investing in artwork, type, printing, paper, promotion and advertising, to say nothing of shipping and such essential nonessentials as foiling and embossing, and really absorbing the entire financial gamble. All he asks in return is an opportunity to get his product displayed and give it exposure to the public, which has the final say on whether or not his bet will pay off. If our major accounts begin to have so much say in what we can distribute, and because of that, in what we ultimately publish, there is no doubt we will see an end to the excitement generated by new products and new talent.

These practices threaten the book industry and writing profession in many ways. For one thing, they intensify the financial pressures on smaller publishers. The house that cannot afford to pay a chain store for featuring its lead novel in the store's catalogue or for displaying that novel prominently will be at a competitive disadvantage. So far, according to one publisher, the smaller houses have responded to the pressure by simply raising the prices of their products. But there is obviously a limit to how much a publisher can charge, and it only postpones the day of reckoning in the paperback jungle. Meanwhile, the consumer absorbs the cost of bookstore positioning, promotion, and display, and higher book prices only force publishers to pay even more money for star authors whose bylines justify those prices.

Thus, the public pays in another way, for the quality of our literature must eventually suffer as publishers gravitate toward the safe, the familiar, and the formulaic. "Small- and medium-sized companies, often hotbeds of creativity, will vanish, or even worse, never come into being," said Zebra's Grossman, "New authors just won't be given a chance. The tried and true, the old and established, will rule—with no successors on the horizon as tastes change or consumers demand something new and different. . . . Whether in the form of slotting fees, trade allowances, or co-op money, this system can only lead to a 'homogenization' of paperbacks, with only 'brand names' and 'safe' titles monopolizing shelf space."

When I was younger and worked for my father during summers in the garment business, I had many opportunities to observe how the wheels of that industry were lubricated. Payoffs and extortion were as common as the pushcarts that crowd the garment district's streets, and very little got done without somebody "schmearing"—the Yiddish word for paying off—somebody else. And after I entered publishing I had reason to feel good about my chosen profession after learning about corrupt practices in such related fields as the movie and record businesses. Perhaps because business on the editorial level is conducted on such a civilized plane, we have come to believe that the same degree of refinement applies down the line in the marketplace where the merchandise is moved. It is somewhat disconcerting, therefore, to learn that such elegant phrases as "sales incentives," "slotting allowances," "co-op contributions," and "display fees," may be euphemisms for something more akin to what is done in the garment business than to the way ladies and gentlemen conduct business upstairs in Editorial.

A bookstore executive to whom I mentioned the analogy pointed out some critical differences. Whereas the list prices of books are printed on the covers, the retail prices of garments adjust themselves in reaction to marketplace conditions. With much wider profit margins available, garment manufacturers have elbow room in which to merchandise their products that book publishers simply do not have. Above all, garment manufacturers do not have the blood-draining problem of returnability that book publishers and retailers have.

We must, therefore, not rush to judgment. The conditions down in the pit are responses to market forces beyond the control of the sales reps and the store buyers, and to some extent, are the result of policies forged in the lofty offices of publishing executives. There are simply too many books for too little space or time, and the brutal laws of supply and demand will not be suspended simply because the product is intellectual or artistic. But as the practices I've discussed seem to be becoming institutionalized on a level uncomfortably close to where the ladies and gentlemen in Editorial live, we should start asking ourselves where we should draw the line between incentives and schmears.

■

Belly-Up

AGENTS DON'T LIKE TO ADMIT THAT there are events beyond their control, and I suspect that is why I have never written more than superficially about such contractual matters as forces majeures—acts of God—and bankruptcy. Such events serve only to reaffirm our human frailty and fallibility, our total helplessness before the awful natural and business convulsions that occasionally devastate the microcosmic world of book publishing. How easy it is to deny that they could ever happen or that there is anything we could do about them anyway. I am able to rationalize my omission of these subjects by telling myself that in the course of my career in the book business, I have never seen a publisher invoke fire, flood, strike, hurricane, insurrection, or war as an excuse for screwing up a book, nor have I or my clients ever been burned by the bankruptcy of a publishing house.

Yet, anybody who works in this business long enough knows that sooner or later Murphy's law will clutch us by the throat, and whatever terrible things can happen will, perforce, happen. These tired old eyes have seen booming markets dry up overnight, seemingly omnipotent chief executive officers of great publishing houses fired ignominiously, and corporate acquisitions, mergers, and divestitures undertaken as casually as cards tossed in a low-stakes poker game.

For instance, some years ago, at the very apogee of the gothic novel boom, Avon, the leading publisher of the genre, announced that it was terminating its gothics program. Snap! Just like that. Writers, agents, and Avon's competitors were floored. It was not as if the market had begun to decline. Anybody who wanted to make a small fortune in those days had but to take anything vaguely resembling a gothic formula story and slap on it a cover of a filmily clad girl looking apprehensively over her shoulder at a fog-shrouded mansion with a light burning in one window. We were all the more baffled because it was said that the head of Avon at that time killed the program simply because gothics bored him, which was like the secretary of the treasury announcing that he is bored with the presses that mint money. But that's what happened, and it left the paperback market in chaos and countless writers and agents floundering around on the wilder shores wondering where their livings were going to come from.

Or, take what happened after Harcourt Brace, the trade and text-book publishing giant, acquired Pyramid Books, an independent and minor paperback house that had suddenly found itself on the map with the huge success of John Jakes's *Kent Family Chronicles*. Harcourt changed Pyramid's name to Jove, replaced most of its staff, and poured millions and millions of dollars into acquisitions and self-promotion in a bid to make it the number one paperback company in the industry. Then, one Monday, the editor in chief and a number of other key editors were given until the end of the day to collect their personal effects and leave the building, and not long afterward Jove was unloaded on what was then MCA's Putnam-Berkley entertainment complex. The upheavals created by these transactions were so immense that few of us had the experience of dealing with anything remotely like it, and the toll on writers, agents, and the industry at large was incalculable. A lot of authors cried, Do something! to their agents, but I can think of scarcely anything an agent might have done to predict or control the situation so that he or she and his or hers would not be adversely affected.

In recent years we have witnessed similarly seismic events. In the space of six or seven months during the mid-eighties, for example, the publisher of Bantam replaced the publisher of Pocket Books, then hired the publisher of Berkley, who quit a couple of months later and presently replaced the publisher of Avon, whereupon the editor in chief of Avon left and was replaced by the editor in chief of Pinnacle. The turmoil caused by these churnings cannot be described. Nor can the harm done to authors be mitigated by the efforts of even the most powerful agents in the business. You just stand there, mouth agape, and watch the majestic unfolding of events. Then you come in when the dust has settled and do what you can to pick up the pieces.

And then, also in the mid-eighties, we witnessed the collapse of a paperback publisher. For many years, Pinnacle Books was a marginal paperback house publishing routine genre books. It was then acquired by an investment group and the old management and editorial staff were replaced by a smart and enthusiastic team that expanded the firm's editorial vision, spent money to acquire better authors and properties, and marketed its books shrewdly and aggressively. Within a year or so the results were dramatic. Sales began to soar and Pinnacle was the hot shop in the industry, a genuine major-league contender. But there were serious problems underlying the successes. The company had expanded so explosively that its cash flow couldn't keep up with demand. Furthermore, as was alleged to me by people close to the situation, Pinnacle's parent company had to "borrow" some of Pinnacle's working capital to cover deficits or corporate acquisitions elsewhere in the conglomerate.

For many of us, the first crack in the structure appeared when a number of Pinnacle's checks bounced. As restitution was made shortly thereafter and cash started to flow again, most of us who'd been touched by that chilly wind accepted Pinnacle's reassurances that the situation was temporary and order would soon be restored. In midsummer, however, agents and authors demanding overdue payments were told that there just wasn't any money. By August the crisis had deepened. Key employees quit or were let go. Inquiries yielded a sketchy but frightening picture of Pinnacle's parent company allegedly using the publisher's accounts receivable to pay off corporate obligations that had nothing to do with Pinnacle. By the end of August the disaster was all but complete: Matters were turned over to the firm's attorneys and the last of Pinnacle's staff was forced to abandon ship.

This was a tragic event. When a paperback publisher goes out of business, there is none to replace it. Mass-market publishers are simply too expensive to create easily from scratch. The loss of a competitor is bad for publishing and worse for authors. The fewer publishers there are, the less flexibility there is in prices and terms available to writers. As if they didn't have it bad enough.

The possibility of an actual bankruptcy sent agents and authors scurrying to their contract files to examine the pertinent provisions of their agreements with Pinnacle. Almost all book contracts contain language to the effect that if a publisher goes or is forced into bankruptcy, takes advantage of any bankruptcy statutes, or assigns its assets for the benefit of creditors, the author is entitled to get his rights back automatically. Examination of the boilerplate of Pinnacle's contract confirmed the existence of such a provision. Specifically, Pinnacle's contract stated that:

> If (i) a petition in bankruptcy is filed by Publisher or (ii) a petition is filed against Publisher and is finally sustained or (iii) a petition for Arrangement or Reorganization is filed by or against Publisher and an order is entered directing the liquidation of Publisher in bankruptcy, or (iv) if Publisher shall make an assignment for the benefit of creditors, then Author may, at Author's option, terminate this Agreement by written notice and, thereupon, all rights granted herein shall revert to Author.

Well, that was a relief. Although we still weren't sure what would become of any royalties Pinnacle might owe, at least there was no question about the procedure for getting our rights back. All we had to do was wait for an announcement that Pinnacle had filed for bankruptcy (or find out for ourselves by sending a lawyer to federal bankruptcy court, where bankruptcy petitions must be filed). Then we send a notice terminating the contract. Right?

Imagine our shock when we learned that the bankruptcy provisions of publishing contracts are, essentially, unenforceable.

I consulted with a lawyer friend of mine, Michael A. Gerber, then professor of law at Brooklyn Law School and now a dean there, who had published a book about bankruptcy, and he cited provisions in the federal Bankruptcy Code that invalidate the bankruptcy termination clauses of contracts. It turns out that book contracts are regarded by Congress as assets comparable to the furniture, typewriters, and light fixtures of a publisher. Section 365(e) (1) of the Code stipulates that an executory contract (that's what you have) may not be terminated just because your publisher goes into bankruptcy. And it doesn't matter whether or not your book has yet been published—it's the contract that counts as an asset.

The reason the law takes this position is that if a company is trying to reorganize in order to work things out with its creditors, as it may do in some bankruptcy cases, its rehabilitation may be hampered if you yank your contracts away. Those contracts are, after all, a key source of potential revenue for a company trying to get back on its feet. Even if a company is not attempting merely to reorganize but is completely liquidating, the law still regards the earning potential of your contracts as an asset to which all creditors have some claim. Thus, you may not get your rights back if the company elects to assume the benefits and obligations called for in your contract. There is some saving grace in all this in that the company cannot keep you dangling interminably. In a liquidation case, the company must decide whether to assume or abandon the contract within sixty days of filing. In a Chapter 11 (reorganization) case, there is no hard-and-fast deadline, but the bankruptcy court may impose one at your request.

So, contrary to the black-and-white language of your publishing contract, if your publisher chooses to take advantage of this provision of the Bankruptcy Code, you're up the creek, at least for a while. Fortunately, few publishers who get into financial trouble go bankrupt because there is usually another publisher waiting in the wings to take it over. A publisher's backlist may continue generating income for anybody who takes it over, and because most creditors of a publishing company (such as a banks, printers, distributors, and the landlord) are incapable of generating income from the publishing of books, sooner or later they will conclude that it makes good financial sense to turn over to a publisher the contracts the creditors control. That is precisely what happened in Pinnacle's case. Electing not to file for bankruptcy, Pinnacle sent a notice to all interested parties stating that it had signed an agreement in principle with the parent company of Zebra Books to take over the imprint. This meant that Zebra would be able to publish certain Pinnacle books under contract or on the Pinnacle backlist.

Back to their contract files scurried the authors and agents, where they confirmed that Pinnacle, like every other publisher, has provisions in its contract permitting it to assign that contract to anyone of its choosing without the author's permission. Some agents and authors are able to modify that clause in negotiations so that a publisher cannot assign the rights without the author's express permission, but most publishers resist that modification, for the freedom to assign is an extremely important one to them, more important at least than it is to authors, for whom it is seldom a deal-breaker. However, even if your contract prohibits your publisher from assigning your rights without your permission, that prohibition would be invalid in a bankruptcy situation under the Bankruptcy Code, according to Professor Gerber.

Actually, the assignment of your contract to another publisher might be the best thing that can happen to you if you are worried that your books may be tied up for years in bankruptcy litigation or seized by some creditor who doesn't know a copyright from a coffin nail. For one thing, before a publisher can assume or assign a contract, it must pay you any royalties it owes you or at least provide you with assurances that they will be paid. Moreover, if your contract is assigned, at least there is someone you can talk to, someone who will keep your book in print and generate some income for you.

That, however, might not necessarily have been the case if Zebra's original plan for taking Pinnacle over had gone through, for the notice Pinnacle sent out stated that the money Zebra generated for Pinnacle would not be paid directly to authors, but would rather go into an escrow account controlled by Pinnacle and its "secured creditor." A secured creditor is someone who has extended credit that is secured by some kind of collateral. In this case, that secured creditor appears to be the bank to which Pinnacle's owners allegedly pledged the publisher's accounts receivable. Authors are not secured creditors. If a secured creditor intercepts revenue that otherwise would have flowed to the company and eventually to you the author, then that secured creditor is under no obligation to satisfy the claims of the unsecured ones. Of course, a judge might be most sympathetic to your plea for return of your rights and royalties, for it is clear that an author is a lot more helpless in situations like this than is a bank or a printer. But a judge is under no legal compulsion to grant an author's plea.

At length, no longer capable of fending off its creditors, Pinnacle filed for bankruptcy under the Chapter 11 provisions of the federal bankruptcy law, meaning it was seeking protection by the federal government while it reorganized and formulated a plan to repay its debts and restore business. It took almost two years, from autumn of 1985 through summer of 1987, for the company to get its act together. It did make a deal with Zebra, which proceeded to review the entire Pinnacle list to decide which unpublished manuscripts it would bring out, which backlist books it would reissue, and which properties it would release to the original copyright owners and under what terms it would do so.

As I said at the outset, agents don't like to admit that there are things they are powerless to control, but I must tell you that bankruptcy appears to be one area where little an agent does by way of negotiating contractual language is going to help if your publisher goes belly-up; and once it does, little that an author, agent, or lawyer does will help if the bankrupt firm and its creditors don't want to cooperate with you. My best advice is, first, to move like lightning once you or your agent get the feeling your publisher is in serious trouble, demanding a reversion of your rights and/or settlement of whatever financial obligations the publisher has to you. Put short deadlines on your demands and send official letters stating that owing to failure of your publisher to comply with the terms of his contract with you, you consider that contract canceled. Second, make a horrid pest of yourself in the hope that your publisher will decide life is too short to do combat tooth and nail with a crazy author.

One author did just that in the Pinnacle case and did win his rights back, but at a terrible cost because of the onerous terms of his settlement and the cost of hiring a lawyer—and you will need a lawyer. But if there isn't that much value in your books to begin with, the cost of hiring a lawyer to rescue them may not be justifiable. It's frustrating as hell, maddening in fact, but there you are. And that's just bankruptcy. I haven't even mentioned how helpless we are before acts of God. But I think I'll wait until a tidal wave demolishes HarperCollins, Random House, or Simon & Schuster before attempting to write about that. Given Murphy's law, you may be reading my remarks about that sooner than you think.

■

Journey to a Small Publisher

T HE FATES OF INDEPENDENT PUB-
lishers in the post–World War II era resemble in their majestic
inevitability the scenarios of Sophoclean tragedies. An established
company, discovering that it can no longer compete for commercially
successful authors, seeks merger with or acquisition by larger and
better financed companies. The management of the smaller company
flatters itself that the new owners covet the vision, intelligence, and
good taste that are the company's hallmarks. To their dismay, they
discover that the only thing their new bosses wanted was the file
cabinet containing their contracts with authors: in other words, their
backlist. In due time, their firm is reduced to an imprint of the parent
company, then ultimately absorbed, dismembered, or liquidated. New
publishers scarcely fare better. At the first sign of success, they are
wooed by flashy and well-heeled suitors, eventually succumb, then
suffer the same destiny as the old-line houses: they die in captivity.

Given this hostile climate, it is comforting to discover independent
publishing companies that seem not merely to have survived, but to
be thriving; have created niches that other publishers cannot easily

emulate; and have resisted the seductive allure of the big-money sellout. One such company is Carroll and Graf (C&G), and I thought you might like to join me on an expedition to its habitat to record the warble of this endangered bird. Though bigger in sales volume and revenue than many other independents, the survival strategies of C&G are fairly typical.

Carroll and Graf, founded on borrowed money in 1982, is a partnership between Kent Carroll, the firm's editorial director, and Herman Graf, director of sales and marketing. The company occupies the third floor of an office building on lower Fifth Avenue. It is by no means lavish; all available space is devoted to the practical task of getting books published. The cost of impressive real estate does not figure seriously in the list price of Carroll and Graf books.

The partners worked together at Grove Press, where they formed a mutual admiration society before launching their corporation. Graf had sold the Grove list nationwide, giving him a feel for the tastes of readers around the country, a virtue often wanting among Manhattan-based publishers who define reality as what plays in the New York media. Graf is also an avid reader whose literary judgment has the respect of his partner. (He was not in town when I proposed to interview them for this piece.)

Carroll, on the other hand, likes to keep his hand in selling and enjoys pitching the list to a few accounts. This overlapping of the partners' activities keeps their company from becoming too editorial driven or too sales driven, either of which can be fatal to a publishing company.

Starting with this harmonious foundation, the partners had to make two important decisions: what kind of books to publish, and how to get them distributed. They immediately recognized that it was suicidal for a new and modestly financed company to compete with major-league publishers for established authors, and they didn't even try. A number of startup ventures in publishing have come to grief because their management thought that the best way to get into the game was to spend money like drunken sailors. Waking up from their binge, the publishers realized that they had exhausted their budget on their first season's list and had nothing in reserve for future operations.

Avoiding this pitfall, Kent Carroll and Herman Graf elected to develop a list of books that might not make an immediate sensation, but would provide a solid foundation for their firm. They started by acquiring the rights to books that they had personally enjoyed reading but which were no longer available. Their shopping list included public domain classics such as works by Balzac, Tolstoy, Conrad, Flaubert, Maupassant, Chekov, James, and Proust; reissues of out-of-print books such as Franz Werfel's *The Forty Days of Musa Dagh,* André Maurois's *Olympio: The Life of Victor Hugo,* and Lion Feucht-wanger's *The Oppermanns;* and secondary or unknown books by famous authors. Looking at Carroll and Graf's catalogue, one wonders how the original publishers could have permitted to go out of print such treasures as Norman Mailer's *Barbary Shore,* John Masters's *Bhowani Junction,* John O'Hara's *From the Terrace,* and several books by G. K. Chesterton.

The partners figured that if they loved those books, many others might love them too, especially a new generation of readers. These classics were available to anyone dogged enough to track them down, they were not that expensive to acquire and, according to booksellers, were very much in demand by readers who could no longer find them in stores. In electing to build its house on a backlist, Carroll and Graf flew in the face of current thinking, which is that the high road to profit is frontlist bestsellers. "There is nothing more valuable than a healthy backlist," Carroll told me. Today, Carroll and Graf has a backlist of hundreds of titles, many of which have been adopted by school systems. It also does a very good mail-order business. "Good books have remarkable lives," Carroll observed. "If mail order is properly done, you can reach a vast audience that cannot be reached in stores, and keep books in print far longer than you can if you restrict your distribution to bookstores."

As for distribution, they selected Publishers Group West (PGW), then a small outfit founded by three Stanford University graduates with whom Carroll and Graf felt a strong rapport. At the time, PGW handled mostly nonfiction and concentrated its distribution efforts on West Coast stores. From the start, Carroll and Graf posted excellent numbers, helping its distributor to become a major vendor to other important accounts. Within two years, Carroll and Graf had become one of PGW's most important customers.

With a solid backlist on which to build, Carroll and Graf ventured on a modest basis into the publication of original books. One of its first books was Nicholas Proffitt's *Gardens of Stone*. When the time came to reprint Proffitt's novel, C&G chose an unusual course. It licensed to Tor Books the right to distribute the mass-market edition in wholesale outlets only (such as supermarkets and airports), and retained the right to distribute it through direct channels, independent bookstores and bookstore chains. "We're very flexible," Carroll says. "We can publish in hardcover, trade paperback, or rack-size, but we can also license those formats if we think it will be better for the book. The author makes the same money, or even more than he would if we were rigidly committed to one approach only, as some bigger publishers are."

Another piece of Carroll and Graf's strategy fell into place when the company determined not to stray too far away from tried-and-true genres. Although there is plenty of room for variety within such categories as mystery and science fiction, the publishers recognized that it was unwise to be too far from accepted genres, "Genre makes the most sense because its costs are predictable," Carroll states, "but low cost doesn't mean low quality. Quite the contrary, some of the most imaginative writers of our time work in areas like fantasy, science fiction, and mystery."

The company backed that viewpoint by publishing reprints of books by such great science fiction, fantasy, mystery, and horror writers as Philip K. Dick, Theodore Sturgeon, J. G. Ballard, Brian Aldiss, Julian Symons, Fredric Brown, Hammond Innes, and John Dickson Carr. It also published anthologies of great stories in various genres, edited by names like Isaac Asimov and Colin Wilson. Little by little, the company stepped up its commitment to publishing originals in these categories. Today, for example, Carroll and Graf does about eight original mysteries per season, often copublishing them with a British house to increase the size of printings and cut down the cost per unit. It also has a very successful list of Victorian classics by that indefatigable erotic author, Anonymous.

The partners do not, however, allow themselves to be blinded by their own successes. Although they are certainly capable of "laying down big numbers," as the industry saying goes, and have printed over 100,000 copies of several books, they know when to walk away from a deal that is getting too expensive.

Authors who get too expensive are a chronic problem for small, independent publishers. They take intense pride in launching the careers of exciting new authors. But it takes very little fresh blood to attract sharks, and soon major publishers are talking telephone-book numbers to the author or his agent. The upshot is inevitable, and it can break the heart of a small publisher who invests too much emotion in the dream of going to the stars with that author. Carroll and Graf did not make the mistake of getting drawn into bidding wars with predatory competitors, and resigned themselves to losing writers they discovered." We lost to the big boys a few authors whose careers we launched," Carroll told me, "but we're not angry. We knew that that's the way the game is played, and we didn't want to stray from our philosophy of keeping within our means." For Nicholas Proffitt's second book, Bantam ended up paying twenty times what Carroll and Graf had paid him for his first. "To Proffitt's credit, he actually hesitated before leaving us," Carroll told me with a smile.

Bantam also figured in a David and Goliath battle over Carroll and Graf's publication of some books by Louis L'Amour. It seems that a knowledgeable bibliophile brought to C&G's attention some old L'Amour works whose copyright had expired, putting them into the public domain where anybody could publish them. C&G checked the claim out and discovered that yes, they were indeed out of copyright. Under no obligation to pay the author, C&G approached him and offered to do so anyway, inviting him to write an introduction.

L'Amour's response, together with Bantam's, was to sue Carroll and Graf. Despite intense pressure and a dreadful drain on its treasury, C&G refused to knuckle under. Today, those books are still in the C&G catalogue. During the prolonged wrangle, however, Bantam rushed the same books into print. Presumably, Bantam paid L'Amour for them.

This portrait of a small publisher stands in vivid contrast to other houses big and small that have fallen on hard times. It is built on a broad and dependable foundation of backlist genre classics, stays with what it does best, avoids getting sucked into expensive and risky auctions, and listens responsively to the voice of its accounts. Though it has grown at a respectable pace since it was founded, it does not aspire to compete in an impossible arena. "We don't see the world from the viewpoint of the executive with ten assistants who makes deals in the Four Seasons," Carroll sums up. "If you go to a certain level, you only increase your administrative and other overhead costs without increasing efficiency or profit. Increased administrative concerns also distract attention from the editorial process. Our low overhead supports rather than dictates our publishing program. We didn't start a company to pay rent. We started it to publish books, to share books we love with people who share our predilections, and we knew there were a lot of such people out there. So I'm not entirely surprised that we've done well."

■

Section Two

Understanding Editors

Editors: The New Disenfranchised

I'VE ALWAYS LIKED EDITORS, BUT I never used to feel sorry for them. That changed when the acquisition of Doubleday was announced.

Until then, whenever I heard that a publisher had been acquired by some sprawling conglomerate, or merged with another publisher, or had simply given up the ghost and shut its doors, my first thought had always been, *This is bad for authors*. The displacement, the disruption, the disarray caused by these corporate earthquakes have been nothing short of calamitous. The publishing landscape of the past thirty-five years is littered with ruined books beyond counting and haunted by the shades of authors whose careers have been maimed and prematurely terminated.

But in the tumultuous last week of September 1986, when deals were concluded for the acquisition of Doubleday and New American Library, my first thought was, How terrible this all must be for *editors*. I spoke to a great many of them after the deals were announced, and I can assure you that few were not anxious and disturbed, if not downright scared. It had finally dawned on editors everywhere that there was no longer any such thing as job security at a publishing company.

What happened to Doubleday was a harbinger of things to come, for, as long as most publishing people could remember, the firm had symbolized bedrock stability—a fortress impervious to the corporate wars that left almost none of her sister-houses unaltered. If anything, Doubleday had bolstered its foundations some years before with the acquisition of Dell Publishing Company, a major paperback house. After the acquisition, the shadow of change darkened the desks of everyone who worked in publishing, and anxiety lurked in every corridor. "Every time my boss buzzes," one editor told me, "I say to myself, 'That's it. They're letting my department go.'" This constant knot in the stomach exists for workers in every area of publishing, including sales, marketing, accounting, publicity, and art.

That the deals were good for the buyers and sellers, few observers question, although there are some aspects that could tarnish the splendor of the prizes. Doubleday's book division had been losing money for some years, owing in good measure (in my opinion at least) to its failure to adjust to the revolutionary change in the nature of our business that made the so-called hard-soft publishers the pre-dominant beasts in the jungle. Indeed, one of the few divisions of Doubleday that was operating in the black, other than the New York Mets baseball team (which they subsequently shed), was Delacorte Press, which had always acquired hardcover and paperback rights together. At the time of the acquisition, Doubleday seldom, if ever, acquired books for its Dell paperback line. Nor did it bend in its rigid refusal to give authors a greater share of paperback reprint revenue than the traditional fifty-fifty split, something that other hardcover houses had yielded to in order to gain competitive parity when bidding for properties against hard-soft houses.

Bertelsmann, the German publishing group that acquired Double-day, also owns Bantam Books, which controls the largest share of the paperback market of any American publisher. The addition of Dell potentially eliminated one competitor from the already shrunken list of paperback firms, and swelled Bantam's market share to a size that some observers thought might attract the attention of Justice Department trustbusters. It didn't, however: monopoly in publishing doesn't yet seem to be very interesting to our government. But a lot of Dell editors braced for pink slips. "I've got my résumés out," one editor told me. "When the other shoe drops, I'll be ready."

If you stood back and simply admired the deal, Viking Penguin's acquisition of New American Library was an excellent one all around. A few years before, Viking had united with England's paperback giant Penguin in order to give both companies stronger hard-soft capability in the United States. But Penguin lacked entry into the critical wholesale paperback market. And so, New American Library, which had been bought by an investment group a few years earlier, was seen as a perfect place for Penguin to enter that market. And Viking would, it was thought, be able to play hard-soft ball in the major leagues.

Ten years later, Penguin's parent company, Pearson Ltd., acquired the Putnam and Berkley groups, and though (at this writing) the various imprints are functioning separately from one another, anyone who has worked in publishing in the last decades of the twentieth century has seen what happens when corporate executives look at their holdings and ask, "Why do we need four companies competing for the same books? Let's eliminate some of them." And poof! Another competitor gone, and more editors canned while the Justice Department sleeps.

Job anxiety had infected the thinking of editors throughout the history of postwar publishing. But because many of you may be too young to have lived through the turmoil of acquisitions, mergers, overhaulings, phaseouts, reorganizations, disassemblies, and absorptions, or for those in the publishing business who are too close to daily affairs to step back and see the carnage through a panoramic lens, let me recite a partial roll call of companies that are no more, or are now just divisions or imprints of the companies that consumed them.

- Appleton-Century-Crofts (a division of Prentice-Hall)
- Prentice-Hall (acquired by Simon & Schuster)
- Simon & Schuster (acquired by Viacom Corporation)
- Atheneum (acquired by Charles Scribner)

- Charles Scribner (acquired by Macmillan)
- Macmillan (acquired by Simon & Schuster)
- Little, Brown (acquired by Time Inc.)
- Warner Paperback (merged with Little, Brown)
- Avon Books (acquired by the Hearst Corporation)
- Arbor House (acquired by the Hearst Corporation)
- Fawcett Books (acquired by Ballantine Books)
- Ballantine Books (acquired by Random House)
- Times Books (acquired by Random House)
- Pantheon Press (acquired by Random House)
- Alfred A. Knopf (acquired by Random House)
- Random House (acquired from RCA by the Newhouse organization)*
- Bantam Books (acquired by the Bertelsmann Group)
- Doubleday (acquired by the Bertelsmann Group)
- Dell Books (acquired by the Bertelsmann Group)
- Basic Books (acquired by Harper & Row, then deacquisitioned)
- Crowell (acquired by Harper & Row)
- Abelard-Schuman (acquired by Harper & Row)
- Harper & Row (acquired by Rupert Murdoch's NewsAmerica Corporation)
- Playboy Press (acquired by Berkley Books)
- Ace Books (acquired by Grosset & Dunlap)
- Grosset & Dunlap (acquired by Berkley Books)
- Berkley Books (acquired by G. P. Putnam's)
- G. P. Putnam's (acquired by MCA, sold to Matsushita, then to Seagram, then to Pearson Ltd.)
- Pyramid Books (acquired by Harcourt Brace, renamed Jove)
- Jove (acquired by Berkley)
- Coward-McCann-Geoghegan (acquired by Putnam, then dissolved)
- Dial Press (acquired by Dell, sold to Dutton)
- Dutton (acquired by Elsevier, sold to JSD, sold to NAL)
- NAL (sold by Times-Mirror to Odyssey Group, resold to Viking, merged with Penguin)

- Rawson, Wade (acquired by Macmillan)
- Silhouette Books (acquired by Harlequin from Simon & Schuster)

This partial list is drawn from a thumb-through of *Literary Market Place,* the publishing industry's directory, and I could certainly go on and on. Taken as a whole, the list represents a pattern of seismic instability so severe that if I were an editor today I would strap myself into my chair just to get some work done.

Publishing is a social enterprise that calls for a large degree of organization, hierarchy, and interdependency, and so, by the very nature of what they do, editors are corporate creatures. It stands to reason, then, that the more attention an editor must devote to matters corporate instead of editorial, the weaker will be his or her attachment to books and authors. The emergence of the superpublisher in our century, a corporate entity whose goals only incidentally have anything to do with the quality of literature and the well-being of authors, has impinged to a greater and greater extent on the time, energy, thought, and care that editors are able to give over to books and those who write them, and as you will infer from the list above, the last couple of decades have raised the level of distraction to critical mass.

The most obvious, as well as detrimental, manifestation of this shift of editors' attention is job-hopping. As their love of books and authors is battered by all the firings and hirings, reorganizations, streamlinings, office politics, shuffling of responsibilities, and the buying and selling of the companies they work for, editors feel fewer compunctions about accepting job offers from other publishers. It's hard to feel company loyalty when corporate logos change with the frequency of automobile styles. Low wages have always prevailed in the editorial profession, but higher pay is not in itself a compelling lure for an editor contemplating a move to another company, unless it is coupled with a promise of greater job satisfaction. But if an editor is not getting such satisfaction, he's going to think a lot about his salary. It behooves us to think about how a $35,000 a year editor must feel when he listens to the complaints of authors making many times that amount. "Few of my authors make less money than I do," an editor told me, "and none makes less than my assistant."

The vicious cycle is accelerated as more and more editors, looking out for number one, jump to other publishers or leave publishing altogether for more lucrative, satisfying, and stable jobs. Even those remaining in publishing find themselves burdened with corporate responsibilities that take them away from what they love most dearly to do—acquire and edit books. Thus, the industry eventually becomes bereft of dedicated editors, and the vacuum is too often filled by people who are more adept at playing corporate games than at developing writers.

In turn, such people place more and more emphasis on buying winners instead of breeding them: acquisition without cultivation. Less and less attention is paid to developing writers; instead, everyone asks how much it will cost to buy and sell them. The publisher that proves itself most capable of acquiring will become the most successful. But the price is dear: When authors are deprived of the time to grow, creativity will be snuffed out. It's as true of literature as it is of agriculture or forestry.

The cycle spins yet faster and higher as other publishers try to emulate the successful ones. Abandoning the philosophy, the tradition, the taste and judgment, and the people that got them where they were, these houses join the chase to try to capture frontlist hits. Even when they snag them, however, they lose a little bit more of their character if not their soul.

The soul of a publishing company is its editors, and when a publishing company alters its fundamental attitudes about books and authors, the sensibilities of its editors must, of necessity, change as well. With promotions and increased corporate responsibilities comes loss of contact with the intimate places in an author's heart where literature is born.

The rest of the editorial staff, as well as the staffs of the other departments that fuel publishing companies, carry on as best they can in the midst of this furious turbulence, but they do so in a constant state of apprehension. How difficult it must be to concentrate, to plan, to pay attention to the work at hand, when upheaval is only one announcement (or even one rumor) away.

Editors today have more in common with authors than they do with the publishing companies that employ them. Both are disenfranchised, both have become fodder for the relentless march of the takeover.

■

Author's note: As I was reviewing the proofs for this book, it was announced that Bertelsmann, owner of Bantam-Doubleday-Dell, had acquired Random House, a company that embraces Alfred A. Knopf, Inc.; Ballantine Books; Crown Publishers; Del Rey Books; Fawcett Books; Pantheon Press; Schocken Books; Times Books; Villard House; and several other publishers.

Must Youth Be Served?

OWING TO SOME CAPRICE OF PROVI-
dence, I happen to have been born on the very same day and in the
very same year as Charles Brown, publisher of *Locus,* the trade magazine of the science-fiction field, in which most of the material in this
book first appeared. Recently, as he and I celebrated one of those
depressing landmark birthdays with a zero suffix, I muttered some
clichés, as aging men are wont to do, about how baseball players and
policemen suddenly seem to be mere children and not the imposing
adults that we once looked up to. Brown's response was, "Editors,
too."

He was right. I don't know whether it's statistically verifiable, but
the trade book business appears, at least, to have become populated
largely by the young, many of whom serve in critically important
executive positions. Despite recent expressions of concern in trade
journals about the industry's failure to attract the young, I haven't
noticed any diminution of college graduates flowing into publishing,
and I'm not terribly worried about it. What I am terribly worried
about is the flow of senior editors and executives and other mature

publishing personnel *out* of the business as a result of mergers, take-overs, reorganizations, conglomeratizations, and internationalizations.

There are few more disturbing manifestations of this turbulent era of consolidation than the departures from our scene of older men and women who have been fired, forced out, or made unwelcome by management. Luckily, I am my own boss, and my prospects for tenure are therefore excellent. But I'm thinking about my many friends in the industry who are not—or were not—as fortunate, and I would like to speak up about the potentially detrimental effects of this trend. I'm not just worried about decent people losing jobs, but about the threat to the publishing business and the very quality of our literature itself.

Publishing has always been attractive to youth. It is not a rigidly organized or forbiddingly hierarchical industry. It has no effective union on the editorial level, no demanding apprenticeships, and the windows of opportunity at the entry and junior levels are pretty much wide open, requiring only a reasonable degree of literacy and office skills. Tasks, at least on the editorial side of things, are not strictly defined, so anyone with a normal measure of ambition and enthusiasm can learn a variety of disciplines, find the right niche, and advance to a middle or even senior editorial level in a matter of a few years. The pay is not great, but the person who sticks with it will find himself or herself in a position of responsibility, if not authority, while still young. Publishing offers young people a chance to apply their ideals to the creation and dissemination of literature. And even after many of those ideals have perished in the crucible of business reality, there remain some compelling attractions for young people: Publishing is glamorous, and it's fun.

Publishers like to employ the young, too. They like their enthusiasm and energy, their sensitivity to new trends and fresh ideas. And it doesn't hurt that young people are a source of relatively cheap labor.

Unlike what happens to workers in many other types of business and industry, the maturation of publishing people is seldom attended by stagnation or decline of vigor, skill, or initiative. Quite the opposite. As they get older, they usually become wiser and more skillful, and their experience becomes a significant factor in the formulation of critical publishing decisions.

Efficiency of performance is one way to define experience. A task that takes hours or days or weeks for an inexperienced person to perform may be achieved in a fraction of the time by someone who has been there often and understands the procedures without having to invest a lot of energy into them. In some undertakings, like the appreciation of literature, the task becomes easier and easier with experience. A senior editor told me, "About once a month a young editor comes running into my office having 'discovered' a fresh story, and I have to tell him that it didn't work in 1955, it didn't work in 1966, it didn't work in 1974, and it didn't work in 1981, and I don't think it's going to work in 1998, either."

From what I have learned about the history of our industry, the founders of the great publishing companies started their careers at very tender ages, but worked far into their twilight years with no diminishment of intellectual potency. E. P. Dutton died in the trenches at the age of ninety-two after seventy-one years in business life. Moses Dodd died at eighty-six, Henry Houghton at seventy-two, James Harper at seventy-four, and so on, and their children and grand-children also lived to relatively ripe ages while extending the power and glory of their predecessors' companies until they became the institutions of today. Of course, living to a ripe old age is not a virtue in itself, but these founders did assemble teams that ran their firms for long, long stretches of time, establishing a tradition of staff continuity that gave each firm a distinct identity. Today, among the many publishers I deal with, I've discovered that those whose staffs have worked together for the longest time are often the most efficient, effective, and responsive to the needs of authors. But such teams are becoming harder and harder to find.

The takeover trends of the last few decades have reversed the industry's reverence for its elder citizens. Coming from orientations very far afield from the publishing business, the acquirers of publishing houses see nothing untoward about mandatory retirement at fixed ages. Examining ways to reduce the overhead of acquired or merged companies, their eyes focus all too quickly on the relatively higher salaries of editors with seniority. Thus, when the axe falls, it falls first on older employees, with little regard for past performance, ability, experience, or any of the other intangible and unquantifiable values such as wisdom and dignity that enhance the life of a publishing house, inspire young editors, and make authors feel at home.

Perhaps the worst by-product of all is the loss of corporate memory that accompanies the dismissal of senior staff members of publishing companies. No matter how much data is storable in computer memories today, the knowledge of how to do things, of what works and what doesn't, of house history and tradition, of where skeletons are buried and dirty linen stored—all this knowledge and more resides in the hearts and hands, minds and souls of employees who have worked for publishers for a long time. From the smallest details of spelling and grammatical usage to the broadest applications of insight into human nature, the memories of mature employees provide untold aid to those who would otherwise have to grope in the dark, often in vain, for the right word, the right information, the right way.

The shunting aside of such people can deal a serious blow to a company's memory the way a blow to an individual's head can cause amnesia. One can reconstruct events from files (if they are still accessible, complete, or accurate), but that can take considerable time. Even then, the recollections that are so vital in formulating a completely textured picture of what happened five or ten years ago cannot ever be conjured out of dead files.

And if, as has been widely asserted, there has been over the last few decades a decline in line-editing and proofreading skills, resulting in an increase in the number of poorly edited books, it may well be attributable to the loss of mature editors and the tradition of professional pride they brought to their work. "I would become physically sick to discover an overlooked typo or grammatical gaffe in a book for which I was responsible," I was told by one retired editor. She went on to say, "Editors today are almost all hired to acquire books, not to edit them. And the books show it. The new breed of editors is undisciplined and uneducated."

64

The same may be said of the decline in the manufacturing arts and skills; the memory and knowledge of how books are made, and made sturdily and beautifully, dies a little bit more with every older publishing person who leaves the field. One art director stated it succinctly when she told me, "They just don't treat books like newborn babies anymore."

Even more tragically, this disregard for the value and values of older people may actually be affecting the kind and quality of literature published today. The impatience that is usually associated with youth corresponds to the impatience of today's publishers to make quick profits as opposed to the more time-consuming nurturing of talent until it develops into a force capable of producing work of lasting significance and loveliness.

The emphasis on youth parallels the emphasis on frontlist publishing, on "new product," on bestsellers. The young editor of today has been raised in an environment dominated by movies, television, and similar technologies whose impact is ephemeral. He or she may therefore be more favorably disposed toward books that offer the quick jolt rather than the delicious lingering immersion into a work of complexity and subtlety, one that challenges the intellect and demands an investment of time. I have seen this vividly illustrated, for example, in the changing nature of humor books, which have shifted from full-length, elegant satires in the Perelman, Benchley, and Thurber tradition, to highly visual quickies, very much akin to comic books or television cartoons.

The seemingly perpetual state of corporate upheaval that characterizes modern publishing has all but fatally undermined the virtue of company loyalty among editors, just as it has among authors and agents. This means that the editor who acquires a book will not necessarily be with the same company when that book is published. The result is a widespread attitude that publishers exist to publish books rather than authors, that authors are only as good as their most recent success or failure, and that a cumulative body of good work does not count for as much as the single breakthrough blockbuster. This attitude is definitely held by many young editors, who almost cannot comprehend the idea of longevity in an era not just of musical editorial chairs but of musical publishing companies. Indeed, you don't have to be a toothless crone to realize the extent to which our business has been vanquished by a children's army. One editor complained to me, "My God, I'm thirty-one, my boss is thirty-four, and he's responsible to a twenty-eight-year-old corporate officer. I've been here eighteen months and no one's been here longer. It's kind of scary!"

The accelerated superannuation of editors threatens to destroy the delicate tradition of honesty, integrity, pride, and manners that has always characterized the publishing profession. And perhaps it is this legacy above all that senior publishing people stand to bestow on the younger generation. While there is much to be said for youth's perpetual reassessment of tradition, the maintenance of the old ways still lies at the heart of the relationship between publisher and author.

■

Tote That Romance!
Lift That Historical!

ARE YOU FLABBY? OVERWEIGHT? Does your muscle tone compare unfavorably to angel food cake? Then I urge you to try the New York Literary Agents' Weight Loss and Shapeup Program. I guarantee that you will drop a minimum of five pounds in two weeks, and by the end of a month you will sport a physique like an Olympic weight lifter. And all you have to do is read!

Here's how it works. Purchase a sturdy leather or canvas shoulder bag or backpack. Fill it with four standard-length category novel manuscripts, or two mainstream novel manuscripts of 85,000 to 100,000 words in length, or one multigenerational saga manuscript 200,000 words long. Add an assortment of book contracts, royalty statements, correspondence, trade publications, a folding umbrella and a pair of Totes, a few complimentary copies of recently published books, a bag containing the pair of shirts you picked up on sale at Bloomingdale's, plus some miscellaneous items such as a bottle of cough syrup, a water bottle, an extra set of batteries for your Walkman, and the tie on which you splashed pesto sauce at lunch. *Important:* the bag must weigh a minimum of fifteen pounds.

At the end of the business day, place the bag over your back or shoulder, and walk from your office to your home, which should be no less than one mile. Stride at a pace of at least three miles per hour, listening to your favorite music on your Walkman. Empty the contents of the bag at home, read it all, repack the bag and schlepp everything back to your office the following morning. Repeat this procedure day in and day out and feel the fat melt away and those muscles rise like volcanoes heaving out of the sea.

In fact, many publishing people in New York—including your faithful correspondent—observe this daily ritual, and though it has become second nature for most of us, I'm not sure that civilians (such as authors) appreciate the prodigies of strength and stamina performed by these unsung heroes and heroines of the editorial world. And, more to the point, it is almost impossible for outsiders to realize just how much literature we consume. I estimate that I log some three thousand manuscript-miles (a statistic officially recognized by the Bureau of Weights and Measures) annually, and read or review somewhere in the neighborhood of 40 million words during that period.

Reading at home is the burden, quite literally, that all publishing people must bear. Except for the occasional emergency requiring us to drop everything to examine a manuscript in our offices, we have to bring work home to read in the evenings or on weekends, away from the relentless distraction of the telephone. Sometimes our bags contain completed manuscripts being turned in under contract by our clients, and other times they bear work by new authors we are interested in. All of this must be devoured in an evening in order to make room for the load that will be awaiting us in the office the next day as surely as the sun will rise. To bear this immense and bulky quantity of paper, a well constructed and capacious bag is necessary. Shopping bags scarcely last a day, and attaché cases are too narrow.

The hauling of literature creates occupational hazards unique to our industry, hazards not classified by any insurance company: Agent's Arm, for example, or Editor's Hip. One of my colleagues swears that years of bringing work home in a tote bag stretched his arms, causing the sleeve length of his shirts to go from thirty-three inches to thirty-four. Backpacks and shoulder bags place serious strain on back muscles. The constant banging of a heavy bag against one's hip has been known to chafe skin and bruise bone. To compensate, I lean away from the bag as I walk, but after straining my back one day I was advised by a doctor that I was in danger of permanently deforming my spine unless I frequently transferred my bag from one shoulder to another or carried a counterbalancing weight to compensate for my fifteen degree heel to starboard. And there's clothing damage, too: bags, buckles, and straps can wear holes in clothing. Most of my slacks are pilly at the place where my bag bounces when I walk.

Needless to say, the most common occupational hazard of all, for publishing people, is eyestrain. We take good care of our eyes, wearing reading glasses if necessary and reading under strong light. Many editors I know reject out-of-hand manuscripts that are printed too faintly or photocopied too lightly, or are printed single-spaced.

I've been spared serious eyestrain because my eyes don't move a lot when I read a manuscript, a practice, I've discovered from talking to colleagues, that is relatively common and is in fact the secret of our extraordinary feats of reading. While many publishing people probably use speed-reading techniques, rapidly scanning line after line, I find that system inadequate for the consumption of a huge number of manuscripts. I read the first chapter or two of a book slowly to get into the story and characters, but then my eyes sort of shift into overdrive. I take in an entire page in a glance, as if I were on a flyby mission photographing it and absorbing the information without breaking the text into smaller components.

Once I get a book's drift, I'm able to turn more than one page at a time, looking in on the story in progress as it were, feeling the pace and texture as I flip and skim. If you think this is not a fair way to evaluate a book, try this experiment: the next time you watch a movie on television, walk out of the room every ten minutes, return after ten minutes, look at the film for thirty seconds, and walk out again. You should have little trouble comprehending and evaluating the film, particularly if it's not a very good one or if you know in advance what it's about from a synopsis in your programming guide.

You can learn a great deal, and often all you need to know, by flipping through a manuscript. If you find dialogue wherever your eyes come to rest, you can immediately determine that the book may be too talky and that there is not enough narrative, description, and action. The opposite symptom, insufficient dialogue, tells me that the book may be dense and ponderous, overwritten or intellectual. My trained eye cruises the avenues of a book looking for sex, and making determinations based on what it finds there: too much, too little, too erotic, too tame.

The technique of scanning or flipping is used not just for work by new authors but by regular clients as well. Although we must, of course, carefully read important books by those authors we represent, some types of books call for less scrutiny than others. Books in a series, for instance: If an author has successfully written six novels in a western series, we can be fairly confident that the seventh will maintain the same level of skill. We already know what it's about because an outline was approved before the author commenced the work. Even so, an agent does well to cast his eyes over a series book to make sure the author isn't getting bored with his or her character, taking shortcuts, or getting careless. Some authors are sneaky types and you can't turn your back on them for a minute.

Of course, the books that all agents and editors live for are those that compel us so thoroughly that we must read every page, every line, every word. Such events are immensely rewarding. The intense emotions evoked by a powerful book, particularly a virginal one in manuscript form, compensate for all the unpleasant things we have to put up with in our business, and it reminds us that good books remain the cornerstone of the publishing industry. But from the viewpoint of a busy agent, such books strain one's eyes as well as one's time. While it may take me half an hour to read and judge a poor book, I need a week of evenings to judge a good one, forcing everything else on my reading schedule to fall behind. And, because absorbing books require one's eyes to move in the traditional reading mode—line by line—I can develop a headache from a good read. Strange, huh?

My wife claims she can tell, merely from the sound of pages

turning, how I feel about the manuscript I am studying. If she hears the quiet rustle of one page every minute, she knows I am interested in it; the sound of clump-clump-clump as I impatiently turn over fifty pages at a time tolls, to her ears, the death knell of a book. My wife suffers with me as I groan with disappointment or curse at wasted talent and effort. Indeed, my wife suffers with me a great deal, particularly at the staggering cargos of reading I bring home with me. "Why," she asks quite sensibly, "don't you bring home just the opening five or six chapters of a book? Then, if you don't like them, you will not have lugged the whole book home for nothing?" The answer is that sometimes a book will get off to a bad start and will only hit its stride closer to the middle. And besides, what do I do if I bring home a partial manuscript and it turns out I adore it? When that happened to one of my colleagues, he got out of bed, threw on his clothes, and hopped in a taxi at midnight to collect the balance of the manuscript from his office, because he simply couldn't wait until the next day to learn how the book turned out.

No, it is not easy being the spouse of a literary agent. "When you lie down with an agent," my wife sighs, "you wake up with paper clips and rubber bands in your bed."

Indeed, I do a great deal of reading in bed, and I hope my clients will not be insulted when I reveal that I occasionally do so with a baseball or football game on the television set. These sports occupy only a few minutes of real time, the rest taken up with actionless hiatuses, time-outs, and commercial breaks. (Basketball and hockey are not good sports to read by because of their nonstop action, and sitcoms and TV movies demand too much listening.) Anybody concerned that I will not pay full attention to his or her manuscript is advised to submit it to me after the Super Bowl and before opening day of baseball season.

I had always wondered whether my reading habits were typical or eccentric, but had never imagined I would have occasion to compare them to those of other publishing people. Thanks to an unusual situation that arose a few years ago, however, I had a rare opportunity to observe some editors in their natural habitat, reading a manuscript.

It happens that a celebrated public figure visited my office and told me about some events in her life that had never been revealed. She then presented me with several chapters and an outline of her autobiography, and they were wonderful. But before she permitted me to submit them, she wanted to impose a condition.

"I'm afraid someone will make photocopies and sell my story to one of those sensational newspapers," she said.

"I will make the editors sign a confidentiality agreement," I assured her. "These are honorable people."

"Perhaps they are, but what about others in the company? You can't control what happens to that manuscript after it leaves your hands."

I raised an eyebrow. "Do you want me to make them read it in my presence and then take the material back from them when they are finished?"

"Yes. Are such things done?"

"Rarely. But in this case I believe editors would go along."

I phoned a number of them, pitched the project, and hinted at the hot stuff they would find in the proposal. When I had their rapt interest, I hit them with my client's unusual condition. With varying degrees of enthusiasm they agreed to it, and I made appointments to visit them in their offices. I was not comfortable with the idea of staring at editors while they read, just as I am uncomfortable when clients gaze at me while I am reading their work. So I brought a book along.

But I peeked.

I had never stopped to think that there may be more than one way to read a manuscript. But as I made my rounds, I was intrigued by the variety of postures, styles, and techniques, and of time consumed in the mundane task of reading. There was the Free Spirit, who tossed each page carelessly onto the floor after she finished it. And her opposite number the Compulsive, who placed each completed page in the rear of the manuscript, then shuffled and tapped the pile to square away the edges before continuing. There was Speedy Gonzales, who whipped through some sixty pages as if it were an Olympic event, and there was the Tortoise, who examined each page as if it were an illuminated leaf from the *Très Riches Heures*. There was the Juggler, who conducted a dozen pieces of normal business while reading, taking phone calls and barking orders to secretaries, and there was Marcel Proust, who rebuked subordinates for whispering while he was trying to concentrate. Yet another turned her back to me, apologizing for being too self-conscious to read while somebody watched her. Some editors sat bolt upright at their desks, others kicked off their shoes, folded their legs beneath themselves on a comfy couch, and sipped soft drinks. I felt like a voyeur.

Some of these editors, after we talked about the project at hand, discoursed on their reading habits. Quite a number take one "reading day" every week or two, staying home to attack the stacks of manuscripts that threaten to evict them from their bedrooms. One told me she runs off photocopies of manuscripts before she brings them home, then throws them away when she is finished so that she doesn't have to lug them back to her office. Another has a system of cookie rewards based on so many manuscripts polished off. We exchanged tips on distinguishing high-priority manuscripts, the ones you have to read before you tackle the less important ones. "I put the important ones on my desk chair, so I have to remove them before I can sit down," said one. "I put mine on the floor *next* to my desk chair so that I have to step over them to get anywhere," said another. "I put mine on my typewriter," said a third. But a fourth topped them all: "I put mine on the toilet seat lid in my private bathroom," she confessed.

And when asked how many books they read annually for pleasure, most of them laughed as if that were the funniest joke they had ever heard. "Reading for pleasure?" one gasped. "What's that?" Another said, "I remember reading for pleasure. I did it once, 1962 I believe it was." Reading for pleasure is an act performed by just about every literate person with the exception of publishing people. I would estimate that I read no more than three books a year that I am not compelled to read by the exigencies of business. The shelf near my bed is jammed with complimentary copies of yummy-sounding books sent to me by enthusiastic publishers. I call it the Shelf of Good Intentions.

But for every one I attempt, I receive ten more. Needless to say, I am cruelly demanding of the books I eventually do read for pleasure. My reading life is too short for anything less than a sublime experience. As soon as I feel my attention wandering, I set the book aside like a friend who has betrayed me and select the next one.

Among the many fantasies I cherish of what I will do when I retire is the delicious one of reading only what I want to read. I will read those books word by exquisite word, with my lips moving. And I will have found heaven on earth.

I just hope I don't go blind first.

■

Publishing, Twenty-First-Century Style

Author? What's an Author?

HOW CAN YOU POSSIBLY CALL yourself an author if you can't process digitized full-motion video signals on your computer, accelerate your image-compression manager to thirty frames per second, and enhance your video with full stereo sound?

The day is coming—and much sooner than you may think—when authors will no longer be able to define themselves simply as creators of literary works. As electronic technology hurtles too fast for even futurists to keep up with, a generation of readers is emerging that will not accept text unless it is interactively married to other media. The twenty-first century's definition of "author" will be as far from today's definition as you are from the town scribe of yore.

The evolution of authors from unimedium creators to multimedia producers has been gaining momentum since the replacement of manual typewriters with electric ones, a phenomenon that any living soul in his or her mid-thirties or older has witnessed. The addition of computerized memory converted these dumb and passive typing machines into utilities possessing the potential for genuine partnership with writers. Each refinement in memory capacity, miniaturization, automation, and audiovisual display exponentially accelerated the typewriter's curve away from mere laborsaving device and toward a purely organic extension of the writer's mind.

At this point in time, we are at a place on the curve where typewriting has been supplanted by word processing, and word processing, in turn, has advanced into desktop publishing. This means that writers are capable of assuming the role of publishers in every function except distribution of their works to the consumer, and even this condition is on the way to being satisfied with the ongoing creation of electronic networks delivering intellectual creations directly to users.

The closer writers come to realizing that potential, the greater will be the pressure on them to expand their skills beyond effectively delivering the written word in print mode. It will be incumbent on them to navigate, and enable computer users to navigate, through a world of sights, sounds, colors, action, information, and special effects. The introduction of the optical disk, with its almost unimaginable memory and versatility, into the writers' repertoire, makes their ascent to the next rung of evolution a foregone conclusion. But what is that rung, and how many others loom above it?

In order to answer those questions, one must have some general understanding of the technological environment confronting today's authors. The current device of choice is the word-processing function of the computer. However, the definition of word processing has been pushed further and further with each improvement in our ability to store and manipulate text. Color monitors, for example, have replaced the early monochrome models, enabling us to employ an incredible array of graphics to supplement and illustrate text. With each refinement, writers have found themselves blessed with options that were almost inconceivable a decade ago.

Technological growth is seldom achieved without a price, however. The same refinements that liberated writers from some kinds of concerns have saddled them with others. Our relationship with text has become complicated, if not obscured, by our need to master new writing tools. More and more of our creative energy has become dedicated to the selection of hardware, software, peripherals, and options. Each improvement challenges us not to become better writers but to become better engineers.

The introduction of the optical disk has only accelerated our momentum in this direction. The vast amounts of information necessary to produce moving images and sound in a computer are digitally encoded by laser and compressed, just as purely audio data is captured on compact discs. The nearly miraculous storage capacity of computer hard drives, floppy disks, and CD-ROMs (compact disc read-only memory) has added to the writer's toolbox two options of staggering power and versatility: interactivity and multimedia capability. Personal computer owners now have the ability to produce not just text, or text accompanied by still graphics, but fully realized audiovisual works. And thanks to the interactive properties of computers, users may now journey through a variety of links that make them active participants in the audiovisual experience.

The problem is, you can't take those journeys with conventional word-processing hardware and software. You can only get there from here by using an "authoring system." An authoring system enables a computer operator to incorporate video and sound into the presentation of creative ideas. Such creations are interactive, allowing the user to cut (nonsequentially if so desired) back and forth from movie scenes to animated graphics to straight text to still graphics to excerpts from documentaries and back again, all accompanied by speech, music, or sound effects.

Authoring systems were created in response to the fiendishly difficult task of programming graphical interfaces into word-processing systems. "Without having to write a single line of computer code, a person can design an endless variety of relatively simple yet functional multimedia programs," says the head of a New York–based multimedia production company. "Technically, the task of designing a multimedia work can now be performed by the average computer operator with nearly as much ease as operating a desktop-publishing program. However, multimedia also offers up a new and unique set of design problems to contend with."

Using an authoring program, you can develop virtually any fully functional application you wish to create. As of this writing, you must still be somewhat computer literate to flesh out your prototype program, but as the systems evolve, using them will become easier and easier.

You'll notice that I am judiciously avoiding the use of the word "author" in referring to creators of such works. That is because the act of creating computerized, interactive, multimedia works is not a function that must of necessity be performed by an author. It's closer to what movie producers do, transforming a variety of media into an integrated audiovisual experience for the viewer. Notice, too, that I say "viewer" and not "reader." For the same reason, the relationship of a user to such works is no longer that of a reader, but is closer to that of a moviegoer, television watcher, or player of interactive video games. Yes, reading may be required when text is involved, but experiencing multimedia goes as far beyond reading text as three-dimensional chess goes beyond the game that is played on a conventional chessboard.

As I acclimate myself to the rich atmosphere of computer technology, I hear the word "author" used less and less and "producer" used more and more to describe those who assemble, integrate, and purvey multimedia software packages to consumers. As the trend toward multimedia accelerates, as I predict it will, the role of the author must, without question, become subordinated to that of the producer. Authors will become scenarists, creating story lines for or textual supplements to full-motion video films for personal computers. The real creative stars will be those who can produce brilliant and stimulating programs for display on home entertainment systems.

Perhaps such individuals should be called "auteurs," the term used for artistic filmmakers who involve themselves in all aspects of making their movies, including writing the scripts, casting talent, directing, and editing. Says one futurist I talked to, "Those who have the vision to incorporate all the elements, and the skill to blend them harmoniously, will be the creative forces in the coming generation of media products."

The application of modern technology to the traditional tools of authorship is going to alter the way fiction is written, and is eventually going to alter it radically. Indeed, one can visualize a day when the term "written" will no longer adequately express the act of creation that conveys an author's vision to the mind of a reader.

An "authoring system" is the generic term for the software used to render these compositions on computers. These systems tie story elements, text, sound, still pictures, moving pictures, animation, and other media elements into a single multimedia package, a piece of software called a "title." The story's scenes and episodes may be linked together in the form of ever-expanding branches, or woven together in something closer to a web. The elements may be mixed and matched, presented sequentially or nonsequentially, separately or simultaneously. Authors can build into the programs a multitude of options for the user to link the elements, alter sounds and graphics (or even create new ones), and influence the direction that the story takes.

The fluidity and spontaneity with which the user navigates around the program resembles the human thinking and decision-making process. For this reason, such programs are referred to as hypermedia rather than multimedia. The content on a movie reel is presented linearly; it can move only forward in time; the viewer's attention is guided by the creator, whose decisions about what happens next are arbitrary and unalterable. In a hypermedia program, the user can access the content in a nonlinear, random way. He can, in other words, elect to go forward, backward, or sideways in time and space, starting anywhere and voyaging as far in any direction or dimension as the imagination of the program's creator, or the technical limits of hardware and software, can take him.

If you're beginning to realize that this changes the relationship between reader and story, you're right. It alters it profoundly. Geri Gay of Cornell University, in an article in *The Hypertext and Hypermedia Handbook,* a McGraw-Hill book, points out that hypermedia "has the potential to allow the reader to become an author of an interactive story." In short, the time is coming when you will not merely "read" a fictional work in hypermedia form, you will be able to collaborate with the author in its creation.

There are a number of systems from which today's would-be hypermedia authors can choose. Because things are moving so fast that these systems may be obsolete by the time you read this, I thought I would create a composite to give you a general idea of how twenty-first-century authors will be telling stories.

Suppose you had an idea for a science-fiction story; a tale of two lovers cruelly separated in time and space. Betty has been abducted by time-warp pirates called Zomboids, and her beloved Edward must search the past, present, and future universe to find her. When he finally gets there, he discovers she has been carried off again, and so on and so on.

The first thing you'll have to do is write a story treatment and screenplay. In fact, if your program is to be interactive, you'll have to write a multitude of scenes branching off from the main story. You'll then have to design settings and sketch visualizations of your characters. As Huk the Hostile, the Zomboid emperor, and his alien buddies are rather protoplasmic (looking like spotted, half-deflated beach balls), you'll use a draw-and-paint package to design them, then animation tools to bring them to life. If you'd like Betty and Edward to resemble your favorite movie stars, you will be able to re-create them identically and three-dimensionally to make it seem as if you captured living actors on film. Or you can film or videotape actual actors. And if, like Alfred Hitchcock, you want to play a bit part in your own movie, you can film or tape yourself, or your kids, or your mother-in-law. Using your movie "toolbox," you'll employ an image scanner to convert still photographs of scenery or interiors into backgrounds, and from your digitized video file you'll be able to splice in some footage from a documentary or feature film, so that it looks like Edward's quest for Betty takes him to third-century Rome, twentieth-century New York, or twenty-third-century Moonbase.

You'll have written some dialogue to depict the bad guys plotting their evil deeds. You'll now record it, using a synthesizer to alter the pitch and timbre of your voice for each character so that you can play all the parts. You can also synthesize the sound effects. The hum of the cruising spacecraft, the howl of entry into Earth's atmosphere, the explosions of warfare, all are reproducible on a synthesizer. Or you can integrate recordings of real sounds into your audio track. The same goes for music.

Although most of these tasks today must be performed on a computer keyboard, or with a mouse, or both, it won't be long before the entire process will be voice activated and you'll simply tell your computer what to do: "Yo, computer. Lights! Camera! Action!"

Now that you've got all your components together, it's just a matter of creating as many scenes as you wish of past or future, so that the user can branch out interactively as Edward chases Huk the Hostile and Betty from one time and place to another. Your program will be so flexible that the user may substitute his own face and voice for those of the characters or enter other elements to individualize the movie. John Markoff, in the *New York Times,* reported a demonstration of a set of Apple multimedia extensions to the Macintosh operating system, in which a user took a video of himself riding a bicycle, then edited it into the final sprint of the Tour de France. In his version, he won the race.

The current state of authoring system art is not as advanced as I have portrayed it. Take the inclusion of video, for instance. Aside from crude home videos, the incorporation of professional-looking video into a hypermedia program is beyond the skill level of today's authors. And even if the technology were closer at hand than it is, you would still need to assemble a movie crew to make a studio-quality video for your title. And the technology is still in a relatively primitive stage. Scientists and engineers have not yet overcome the difficulty of compressing onto disks the immense amount of information necessary to display an abundancy of visual images, especially moving ones. Thus, most hypermedia titles today are heavily text oriented, or "hypertext," to use the phrase coined by computer guru Ted Nelson. Animation is currently the "motion picture" of choice, as it is more manipulable than video for the purpose of interactivity. But extensive animation also requires a digital density that is, at present, beyond the reach of most home "auteurs."

You can see from this brief tour that there is practically no resemblance between the activities of conventional writers and those of the individuals producing works of hypermedia. Let's look at the distinctions a bit more closely.

As you begin to design your scenario and screenplay, you'll immediately be struck by a profound realization: you no longer need the narrative skills you depended on when you wrote books. Although the first crude CD-ROM adaptations of fiction were narrated stories illustrated with still pictures or short segments of video or animation, it was quickly realized that a new art form had been born. Because you are in effect making movies, the descriptive powers you used to call upon to create vivid prose images for your readers are of practically no value at all. You have become a screenwriter: those vivid images will not be portrayed in words but in pictures. And because it's much harder for a viewer to juggle a lot of expository information than it is for a novel reader, the stories you develop for your hypermedia programs are probably not very elaborate or subtle.

It won't be long before you realize that your storytelling expertise is of far less importance than your engineering abilities. Good novelists often talk about the way their books play like movies in their heads, and how they construct their scenes in their novels the way screenwriters construct scenes in films. Well, now you novelists will have a golden opportunity to convert those mental images *literally* into motion pictures. But the technical challenge may be far beyond your capabilities. Even more importantly, it may be far beyond your interest. Many of you facing these options will say to yourselves, If I'd wanted to be a screenwriter, I'd have gone to Hollywood, or, If I'd wanted to be an engineer, I'd have gone to Rensselaer Polytechnic Institute. You wanted to be a novelist.

Many writers must be wondering if there will be any market for their skills in the hypermedia age. I believe there will be. Students of technology are fond of pointing out that the advent of movies didn't destroy our taste for reading, and the advent of television didn't destroy our taste for movies. The advent of hypermedia will not strike a fatal blow to conventional literature written and published in the conventional way. "The technology to create hypermedia is available to authors who want to use it," one multimedia producer said to me. "I don't, however, think that in the near future, someone lacking the skill to create hypermedia fiction is going to be out of work." However, future authors who are not hypermedia/multimedia literate may well be at a disadvantage.

The prospects for readers may be brighter than they are for writers. With information presented in such graphic, colorful, and entertaining forms, the rewards of reading for pleasure may well give way to the joys of navigating through a multimedia program, experiencing fantastic audiovisual effects that readers never got out of old-fashioned books or even old-fashioned movies. And scholarship has become more fun now that, instead of having to trudge to a library and drudge at a desk, the library can be summoned by the touch of one's finger on a key or mouse, or by voice command to one's computer. And all that scholarly information is being presented in ways that are a delight to the eye and ear.

The revolution will not stop with the eye and ear. In a more distant future, the development and refinement of virtual reality technology will eventually tie in with hypermedia, bathing all of our senses in experiences that are all but indistinguishable from reality. From there it is not inconceivable that we will tap directly into the human brain, realizing a vision long cherished—and dreaded—by science-fiction writers.

Returning from the sublime to the mundane, we realize that the advent of hypermedia presents some genuine challenges to the traditional ways that intellectual property has been protected. What, for instance, happens to your copyright when a computer user creates a new ending for your story? Does it become a new work? Is it possible that this new work could be copyrighted as a collaboration between yourself and the user? And remember how you used the faces of a pair of famous movie stars when you created Edward and Betty? Did you have the right to do that? Whose faces are they, anyway, the stars' or the re-creator's?

Clearly, copyright in the twenty-first century will be a minefield. Thus, for authors who fear being thrown out of work by the electronic publishing revolution, I have good news: there will be lots and lots of job opportunities in the field of copyright law. Although you will, of course, first have to get a law degree, I can guarantee no end of challenging cases, protracted litigation, and chances to write new law. The seven-league strides made by scientists and technologists in electronic information have left lawyers in their dust. If they don't catch up, the protection of intellectual property will be a shambles. It is already dangerously unstable.

Among other purposes, copyright law was designed to protect the creations generated by the minds of authors, at least for enough time so that they and their heirs may profit from its dissemination.
Until the 1960s, the device commonly used to reproduce those creations was the printing press. The printing press is a large, cumbersome, and expensive machine that is beyond the means of most people to own and operate, even if they were inclined to do so. But that is what you would have had to do if you wished to make a copy of a book or story instead of purchasing it in the marketplace. A pirate, such as a publisher in a foreign land that was not a signatory to various international copyright conventions, could profit from running off a lot of copies of someone's book, but it made no sense for private individuals to do so. Oh, there was the mimeograph, the poor man's version of the printing press, but it required you to retype the item you wanted to reproduce. If you actually wanted to copy a literary work or document, you had to take it to a photostat shop where it was photographed one page at a time. The resulting product was white type on a black background on shiny, stiff photographic paper. It was easier and cheaper just to go out and buy the book or magazine than to go to such enormous trouble. Either that or steal it from the library.

The advent of the photocopier changed all that, bringing the capability for private reproduction of literary work into every home. The first such machines, made by Xerox—I wish I'd saved mine as it will be a valuable collectible one day—were primitive variants on the photostat, using light-sensitive coated paper to reproduce a page placed over a lighted screen. Although it was too crude to run off reproductions of any quality, and too slow to run them off in any quantity, the machine did bring copiers into the home.

The rapid refinement of "xerography" created an industry of local photocopy shops that can run off infinite copies of literary works of a quality equal to that of the originals. Most customers did not realize there were laws protecting the works they brought to the copy shops, and if the operators of such shops were aware they might be violating copyright statutes, they certainly didn't take any measures to locate or compensate the copyright owners. They probably didn't think it was their responsibility. Publishers became more and more alarmed, however, as copy shops brazenly reproduced work that those publishers had licensed on an exclusive basis. Though they eventually succeeded in compelling the largest chain of copy shops to observe proper copyright clearance procedures, the ignoring of copyright law is still widespread in the copy shop industry.

I suppose it could be brought under control through more assiduous monitoring. But the copyright problems created by another technology, personal computers (PCs), make copy shop operators look like Talmudic scribes by comparison. This time, the perpetrators are you. If you own a computer, you may be breaking the law, perhaps flagrantly.

In a nutshell, the problem is that for a modest outlay of money, you can acquire the technological means to copy any image or text without permission of the creator or copyright owner. You may then alter it on your video display screen as if it were a work that you yourself had created. And you may then print, publish, broadcast, or otherwise disseminate it. And make money doing so.

Scanners, for instance, capture published text and transmit it digitally into the memory storage of your computer. Another invention, compact optical disks, enables you to edit, change, or otherwise manipulate that text. Other technologies exist for storing or generating pictorial material and for retouching it or blending it with other pictures into a composite, thus changing the meaning of the original. Advances in the compression of information on disks via lasers make it possible for you to stock your PC library with literature you did not get permission to copy, possibly making you a thief, and to make and sell copies of those works, possibly making you a pirate. You may transmit those works electronically across interstate and international telephone lines, possibly making you a larcenist.

Of course, we rebel against such characterizations. Why? Because the means to capture, store, and manipulate information electronically have become so easy for computer owners that it feels like a natural right, like the right to breathe air. And indeed, this sense of entitlement taps into another aspect of copyright law, the public's need for easy access to creative and intellectual works. Because the doctrine of "fair use" for educational and related purposes supports a degree of free access to otherwise protected texts, we feel few qualms about photocopying a copyrighted article, story, poem, or book excerpt at a copy shop, duplicating a movie on our home VCR, or taping a favorite tune and running off recordings for our friends. Even those of us in the authoring, agenting, and publishing business who would howl if someone pirated our copyrighted text scarcely give a thought to the legal and moral implications of these deeds when we commit them ourselves. But many others have begun to think and talk about them, and to try to formulate rules and standards that reassert control over a body of statutes that grows more irrelevant with each day.

The heart of the problem is that, because of the difficulty of distinguishing between content and the modes of display, the media have become harder and harder to define. Are you stealing somebody's story by simply displaying it on the screen of your personal computer? Are you publishing that story by transmitting it over a computer network onto somebody else's screen? Do you become a co-author when you alter someone else's text?

The copyright law only confuses the issues further. A work of authorship is protected as long as it is "fixed" in a "tangible medium." A book is, of course, a tangible medium that is fixed on paper, but can we say the same about the *image* of a book on a computer monitor? And though the law states that a copyright owner has the exclusive right to "reproduce the work in copies," the law also makes it clear that *displaying* a work does not amount to reproducing it, even though it might well be said that the work is fixed in the program of your computer. In 1980, the Copyright Act was amended to make sure that we understand the difference, defining a computer program as "a set of statements or instructions to be used directly or indirectly in a computer in order to bring about a certain result." In other words, the medium is not the same as the message. Yet, the blurry line between the two is creating no end of vexations for those trying to apply old rules to unprecedented situations. This explains why legislation redefining copyright (as well as trademark) in the computer/Internet era has been stalled in Congress. And the explosive growth of the Internet combining a deluge of text with one-click copying and disseminating capabilities has made the problem absolutely nightmarish.

Private use of copyright information is one thing, but deliberate and methodical theft is another, and the impossibility of policing abuses has severely damaged the economic value of intellectual assets by as much $60 billion by some estimates. Illegal publication of books overseas, for instance, costs American publishers about $1 billion annually. Pirated videotapes of Hollywood films may be costing the movie industry as much as $6 billion a year. Because it is fruitless to go after individual users, particularly in light of allegations that some foreign perpetrators are protected by their governments, the burden of restriction has fallen on the manufacturers and distributors of hardware and software. This takes the form of antitheft devices built into computer hardware and antipiracy instructions programmed into software. The increased costs of such protection have been passed along to consumers.

The computer software industry has also called on patent law and trade secrecy statutes. The so-called shrink-wrap license treats software as a trade secret: the act of opening a package of software is supposed to legally commit you to maintaining the secrecy of the program. The literature that accompanies the package presumably binds you to a pledge not to "use, copy, modify, merge, translate, or transfer" the software without the express agreement of the manufacturer. These oaths are commonly ignored by most consumers and gleefully flouted by hackers.

Concerned observers have created organizations dedicated to addressing these issues and formulating new standards. New York University's Interactive Telecommunications Program (NYU/ITP), for instance, established a Division on Copyright and the New Technologies aimed at defining the problems and creating sensible and effective copyright policies that balance reward for creative work with the widest possible dissemination of these works.

Donna Demac, former director of the NYU/ITP division, wrote in its prospectus of her concern that we may soon be unable to differentiate between "impermissible clones and legitimate derivative works," and that "the issues of ownership and originality are pivotal to the future development and profitability of new services." But many, she warns, "believe the technology to be on the side of unbridled access."

A number of organizations are trying to address the concerns created by the new media, developing programs of research and education, producing archives in various media, and conducting workshops, seminars, and other forums for the airing of the issues, and bringing them to the attention of Congress, industry, schools, and other institutions. Hopefully, these efforts will result in a new set of standards that will restore our feet on firm ground in this exhilarating, awe-inspiring, frightening, new electronic world.

■

Techno-Agents

Nowadays, whenever literary agents get together, the topic most likely to be discussed is not, Which Hollywood agent do you use? but rather, Which computer system do you use?

Recognizing the necessity of organizing their records more efficiently and accessing them faster, most agents have joined the electronic revolution and acquired computers. And, like so many other businesspeople, they have discovered that the blessings of computerization often stay only a few steps ahead of the curse.

The challenge of computerization is not entering data but thinking about it, and I can personally testify that not all literary agents are as good at thinking about data as they are at thinking about big advances, high royalties, and expensive lunches. Luckily, when I decided to overhaul my agency's systems, I had the wisdom to hire some technical consultants who were so smart it was scary, and to employ associates who speak computerese as naturally as they speak publishing.

I am going to discuss the challenges that confront an agent

interested in creating a computer program and database. But before I do, I think it's important for you to know that agents who keep their records on computer do not necessarily have an advantage over those who still rely on traditional manual recordkeeping. For one thing, a literary agency's computer system is just as susceptible to the garbage in/garbage out syndrome as that of any other business. And, for another, the nature or volume of an agency's activities may make computerization unnecessary. I have an agent friend who represents a small number of clients, but they are among the top moneymakers in the publishing game. One day I asked him which computer he used.

"I don't," he said.

I was shocked. "But . . . how do you keep track of all those royalties?" I gasped.

"We never get any."

"Huh?"

"The advances I get are so big, they never earn out royalties," he explained. "I just need to keep track of the advance installments. That can be done on three-by-five cards." His smirk was so obnoxious, I made him pay for lunch.

The time for an agent to begin thinking about computerization is when the volume of paperwork becomes so great that it begins to create inefficiencies, delays, and errors. If the company is not too old, the conversion can embrace the backlist as well as new deals. If the agency is an older one, however, decisions must be made about where to cut off the records on old books. Some firms draw an arbitrary line on the calendar and decide that everything after a certain date will be computerized, everything before will continue to be maintained manually. Others select certain backlist titles that have an active history of royalty earning, and fold them into the records of current and future titles, leaving the dead wood on file cards. Occasionally, I discovered, dead wood bursts into flame as books that have not been heard from for years suddenly earn royalties. For these we made computer entries and they are now permanently in our electronic files.

The conversion of an agency's recordkeeping from manual to computer can create some serious turmoil. If the agent or his staff is inexperienced in data processing, it means learning new skills, languages, and ways of thinking. Most agents are so busy conducting business that the time to learn and practice on the computer, and then to enter all that data, is extremely limited. Clerical personnel who are incapable of handling the technology may become "redundant," to use a British euphemism. These days, agents advertising for clerical help demand to see computer skills on the résumés of job candidates, and, happily, most young people coming into the publishing business seem to have been born clutching laptops.

The activities of literary agents are unique in many ways, and there is therefore no user-friendly packaged program on the market for them to simply boot up and start using at once. And besides, every agent organizes his records in his own way. As a result, all of the programs employed today are hand-designed. Many agents bought or copied their programs from other agents, then adapted them to their own methods of running their businesses. I cannot say that one system is superior to another, but there are certain types of information that all agents must process, and only so many ways of organizing them. I will draw on experiences common to many of my colleagues as well as my own in explaining to you how we approach the challenge of computerizing our records.

A great deal of agency recordkeeping is essentially a glorified form of listmaking, and listmaking is a piece of cake for word processors. Creating client lists, setting up manuscript delivery schedules, tracking book orders, and generating address directories are examples of basic lists that require little thinking or technical skill on the part of the computer user. And even more sophisticated functions, when you analyze them, are little more than lists. Setting up a file for a complex multibook deal with payout schedules as long as your arm is nevertheless a variety of the basic list. In short, an agent could easily get away with a simple word-processing program for much of its record-keeping. At least, at the outset.

The game becomes more interesting when one begins to ask more of the system than mere lists. Let's look at some of the data we have to wrestle with. There are two major classifications of information we must process. The first is that which relates to our clients' business; the second relates to our own. How much money an author is owed by his publisher, when we collect it, and how much we disburse to him, are pertinent to the interests of our clients. The tallying of our commissions, our disbursements for payroll, rent, office supplies, and other overhead costs are of concern only to our accountants and ourselves. These two classes of information are independent of one another; they do not necessarily have to be tied together on the computer. In fact, tying them together boosts the data-processing headaches to a much higher and sometimes nightmarish level. For several years, my agency posted its client records on computer, but wrote its accounting ledgers out in the old-fashioned method, by hand. If an author wanted to know how much money we had collected for him in any given year, we could accurately produce a printout for him in five minutes. But if our accountant wanted to know how much money our agency had earned in that same year, our bookkeeper had to tally up handwritten ledgers on an adding machine for hours. When we finally decided to computerize our agency's accounting system and tie it in with client bookkeeping, the technical difficulties multiplied exponentially. Among other things, we had to buy a more powerful computer, hire a more experienced bookkeeper, install an accounting software package compatible with our accountant's, and convert our check-writing system from one done by hand to one that issued checks on a laser printer. But I shan't bore you with all that. Let's talk about you.

When your agent sells your book, he must set up a file in his computer summarizing the basic deal points (advance, payout schedule, royalties, territories) and other vital information. This will enable him to review the important elements of your agreement without having to search for the contract in a file cabinet. He will also have to create a separate schedule of advance installments so that he can track money due from your publisher. In most cases, advances are payable in more than one installment: upon signing of the contract, upon delivery of the manuscript or revisions, upon publication, and even beyond publication.

Some agencies have two separate files to cover payments immediately due and those that are not due until some future event triggers them, such as delivery of a manuscript or publication. By querying the computer, your agent can summon a list of all monies due now, later, or both.

When your agent collects an installment of your advance, he has to enter the data in a variety of computer files. First, it goes in the file for that particular book. Anytime he wishes to know what's been paid over the history of that contract and when, he can check the author's file by title. Second, there has to be a file listed under the author's name. This enables your agent to review monies he has collected for and remitted to you over the lifetime of your association. It also enables him to promptly answer questions about past payments. Finally, it enables him to report to you about your earnings in any given year, for tax purposes. This particular file can be tied in to a program for issuing 1099 forms to authors as well as to the IRS, in order to verify income.

The processing of your check must reflect a variety of calculations: the gross amount, your agent's commission, and recovery of out-of-pocket expenses such as photocopies, messenger services, or loans. Such charges are listed in a separate file and must be pulled up before your check is cut. Your agent may keep a separate file for allocating commission shares to employees who work for him on a commission basis.

The calculation of foreign revenue is a particularly aggravating job. Those of you who love to program will find much to occupy yourselves with in producing a formula for calculating the foreign gross (converted to U.S. dollars) less the foreign agent's commission, less any foreign taxes, less charges for transferring the money to the United States, less the U.S. agent's commission, and less any expenses your agent recovers. This mathematical legerdemain must then be translated into reports or disbursement statements that the author can understand.

Agents are finding new ways to exploit the inherent potential in the computer, employing it for such functions as flagging expiring options, contracts, or terms of copyright; automating notices (Where are the author's copies? Where are the contracts? Where is the money?); creating a host of databases (subsidiary rights sold, lists of editors interested in cat books, etc.); and producing documents such as collaboration agreements or film options. Scanning technology enables us to store images of contracts and other important documents on disk or in the hard drive of our computers, enabling us to access them in moments, locate provisions instantly, and create a variety of databases and boilerplate language. Using fax and online features of our computer, we can deliver copies of these documents at the stroke of a key. The savings in file cabinet space alone, especially for those of us living in New York City, for which the phrase "high-rent district" was coined, are worth a king's ransom.

The benefits to authors as a result of improved information gathering and processing on the part of their agents is obvious. But the critical question is whether agents will be able to utilize their computers not merely as tools but as weapons in their struggle to improve the lot of their clients.

It's clear to me that the answer is yes. The most obvious reason is that if agents are not snowed by paperwork, they will be able to attend more promptly and effectively to their number one job, selling books, and their number two job, chasing publishers for contracts, statements, and money. The 59 minutes and 30 seconds I save on a hitherto hour-long job of shuffling through activity cards or pulling a file out of a cabinet and examining every document in it is time spent making a phone call or attending a meeting. That makes me a better salesperson and a better watchdog.

And, utilizing the word-processing features of our computers, we can issue dunning letters more promptly than ever before. One program, Rights Only, was developed by Dan Dixon of the University of California Press to aid subsidiary rights directors of publishing companies (who perform many of the same functions that literary agents do) in the management of their lists. Rights Only not only offers a comprehensive database on rights available or sold, but *automatically* issues reminder letters to delinquent publishers on dates when decisions, contracts, or money fall overdue. SKP Associates, a New York firm headed by Sandra K. Paul, has been enhancing and adapting Dixon's program for literary agents. The potential for improving collections is obvious.

Information is power, and the agent who can gather, organize, and apply information more efficiently may well be able to match the advantages that publishers currently enjoy over authors. I can easily foresee a day when agents will be able to access publishers' records pertaining to their authors' books. The instant availability of printing, distribution, and reserve data can only confer more clout than ever upon literary agents.

This vision is all well and good, but some of us have a long way to travel before we can realize it. The agenting profession has its share of technophobes just as any other line of work does, as I discovered one day several years ago when I visited an agent to see her newly installed computer system. Beaming with pride, she had her book-keeper put it through its paces, and I was deeply impressed. When we were finished, I turned to her. "Can you operate the computer yourself?"

"Sure," she said. "I just press 'Bringme.'" She waggled a handful of long, beautifully manicured nails.

"'Bringme'?"

"Yes. I decide what information I need to know. Then I press this button here"—she indicated the intercom on her telephone—"and I say 'Bringme.' And someone brings it to me in two minutes. It's amazing!"

■

What's New? Don't Ask!

AS A BUSINESSMAN, I TRY TO KEEP up with technological advances in order to maintain an acceptable level of service and efficiency, and to keep up with the competition. My agency has computerized its record- and bookkeeping systems, acquired state-of-the-art word processors, overhauled its primitive (early nineties) telephone system, and was among the first in its field to develop a Web site. So, I don't think anybody can accuse me of hostility to the march of progress. Yet, some recent applications of electronic technology have made me feel like little more than a well-dressed allosaurus and left me wondering whether the publishing business as we know it will be recognizable by the end of the century, or even the end of the week. Though many of my agency's authors make their livings speculating on the fantastic, I'm not sure that even science-fiction writers are aware that current techniques of writing, producing, and distributing books are transforming with breathtaking speed. If they don't keep up, writers may end up in the same tar pit as literary agents.

For example, not long ago, the mailman delivered to my office the catalogue for the list of books scheduled for a newly created publisher. The printed catalogue was typical as printed catalogues go. But it was accompanied by the first—to my knowledge—book catalogue produced on videotape. Anybody interested in learning what this house was up to could not only browse through its publication list, but see its titles presented live and in color on videocassette. MTV has come to the world of books.

Some twenty-one works of fiction and nonfiction are introduced in the video catalogue, utilizing a television magazine format. There are interviews with authors, dramatizations, pictorial exhibitions, and other imaginative techniques. While most publishing people skim catalogues in a matter of minutes, the video format tantalizes your curiosity from book to book, making it hard to reach for the fast-forward button. Even more significant, while many of the same books in a conventional printed catalogue might be forgettable, every title in the video catalogue made a memorable impression on me. Some of those books are undoubtedly midlist, but they all felt like lead titles.

The video catalogue approach offers an interesting and considerably less expensive alternative to the elaborate sales conferences conducted semiannually by the most important publishers today, and it might one day replace the travelling sales representative. If other publishers follow this publisher's lead, we may see dramatic changes in the way that publishers display their wares to the book trade.

Another innovation utilizing up-to-date technology combines the television and telephone to promote books. Your favorite author appears on a cable television commercial and pitches his new book, inviting you to call a certain 900 telephone number to hear his recorded message. After seeing and hearing the pitch, you trot out to your local bookstore to buy the book.

At first, hearing this may not sound particularly revolutionary to you. But suppose I told you that the campaign doesn't cost the publisher a penny. And that the author could earn a royalty every time somebody calls to hear his message. (I knew that would get your attention!)

The commercials are not paid for by the publisher. They are

financed and produced by commercial firms entering into joint ventures with the telephone company. Calls to 900 phone numbers are billed to the caller, and the revenues generated by the calls are shared by the producer and the phone company. At current tariffs, a call to a 900 number will cost you $2 for the first minute and 45¢ for each minute thereafter. If 100,000 callers respond to a televised pitch and call that 900 number, they will generate a minimum of $200,000. It doesn't cost the publisher anything except a bunch of promotional copies, which are then autographed by the author, to be given away to the first callers, or some similar promotional purpose. After recouping the cost of producing the televised commercial and recording the phone messages, the producer might pay a royalty to the author (if the author is smart enough to negotiate one). And of course, the author stands to earn royalties on copies of his book sold to bookstore consumers stimulated by the 900 campaign. It's a no-lose proposition for both publishers and authors, and when I recently proposed it to a publisher, he was dumbfounded. He kept asking me, "So what's the deal? So what's the deal?" expecting me to say there was a hidden cost. There isn't.

In fact, there is actually a hidden benefit. Employing state-of-the-art telephone technology, the producers of 900-number book commercials are capable of surveying callers to obtain vital demographic information. In other words, the producers can get a profile of the book buyer-caller, making it possible for perhaps the first time in the history of the publishing industry to quantify the location, age, income, tastes, and habits of the people who buy books. This data can be applied to help publishers focus on their markets with unprecedented accuracy. The publishing industry is so unused to market surveys that when I called several publishers requesting a list of questions for use in such polls, they confessed they had not given the matter very much thought!

Nor had it occurred to them that they too could exploit the 900-number concept to sell books. In that scenario, the commercials would be sponsored and produced by the publisher. Callers would not merely listen to a message but would be able to purchase the book on the phone, charging it to their credit cards or even their phone bills, cutting cumbersome traditional book distribution systems out of the seller-to-buyer loop.

If a number of technologists have their way, publishers themselves may be cut out of the loop. They have been creating, in the words of J. Neil Schulman, "the first fundamentally new way of publishing literary works since Gutenberg invented movable type." This approach is to acquire rights to literary works and transfer the text to disk. The texts are then offered to subscribers. They may acquire the disks through the mail, or have the text transmitted via modem directly into their personal computers. Subscribers pay a basic fee for a software program that provides decryption procedures, to protect the work from tampering or piracy.

Interested "browsers" may read about available titles online, and can order the works for about the same price as that of a mass-market paperback. They may then read the books onscreen, or have them printed out using a word processor and printer. Every time a subscriber purchases a title, the fee is shared by server and author according to a previously negotiated formula. The "publisher" ("provider" may be a more accurate term) accounts to the author on a monthly basis, and of course there can be no reserve against returns because there are no returns.

Schulman's philosophy is that authors have always dreamed of transmitting their work to readers "with as little mediation between them as possible." Obviously, the mediating entity currently standing between author and reader is the publisher, and because of the cost and complexity of book editing, manufacture, warehousing, distribution, and promotion, this form of intervention in the transmission of text is highly inefficient and unprofitable—a fact that should come as no surprise to anyone remotely familiar with the publishing trade. Electronic publishing (or, more accurately, electronic packaging, since servers or content providers don't actually publish) challenges every assumption on which the publishing industry currently rests. The new technique eliminates the need for bookstore shelf space; startup costs and the attendant risks are sharply reduced; the lengthy time between delivery of a manuscript to a publisher and publication date is slashed to something close to thirty days; and the costs of manufacture and storage are negligible. Fulfillment of orders is immediate and perfect, and there is no speculating on how many copies to print, since one copy is printed per order. There is no such thing as out-of-print titles, nor remainders or destroyed copies. The shipping cost per unit on disk is about the same as what it costs to mail a letter first-class, or, for download via modem, the cost is borne by the consumer ordering the book.

As I mentioned earlier, this approach, called "publishing on demand," takes advantage of a number of exciting technological developments. Word processing, for instance, enables authors to produce their work on software that is compatible with the server's. Even if it is not, printed text can be machine-read by scanners and thus translated onto disk. Modems enable the packager to transmit the work over the telephone. Not only can the work be downloaded via modem onto the buyer's computer, but it can be re-created in a variety of ways: onscreen, printout, voice synthesizer, or, one day, pocket-sized electronic "book players."

Editing remains the responsibility of authors, but there are few authors who have not boasted that they can do as good a job at editing as their publishers. That assertion is bolstered by software packages enabling authors to desktop-publish their own work with attractive book design and typeface, and with built-in grammar and spelling-check features. Or such functions will be undertaken for a fee or percentage of revenues by the packager. The same goes for advertising. The reviews can be posted on electronic bulletin boards of subscribers or would-be subscribers, who might also be offered free excerpts of works in which they are interested.

Are these truly ideas whose time has come? Well, if you think of them strictly in technological terms, that may well seem true. But many a great invention has gone unexploited because it didn't take into account human nature, psychology, and customs. The fact that these applications have been developed doesn't necessarily mean they will take.

Consider that video catalogue. It certainly had a powerful impact on me. But it also took forty-five minutes to run through all of its titles. Most publishing people I know don't have nearly that kind of time. It takes five or ten minutes at most for someone in the book trade to read a printed catalogue. If all publishers put their catalogues on videotape, there would simply be no time to do anything else. When would agents be able to go out to lunch? When would editors find time to send their résumés around? Remember that major publishers have a lot more than twenty books on any given seasonal list, and that doesn't include the backlist, which can number thousands of titles. The video catalogue may have its place as a supplement to bookstore or sales conference presentations, but it won't replace the printed catalogue entirely.

The use of 900 telephone numbers to promote books is certainly ingenious and, on the surface, irresistible. Ask a publisher if he would like to see his books advertised on television free of charge and he will kiss your feet. Ask an author if he would like to earn royalties on his recorded phone messages and he will kiss just about any part of your anatomy you may designate. But does the 900-number concept work in practical terms? Early experience suggests it works only for a very limited type of book. The cost of producing the commercials and phone messages and buying air and telephone time are prohibitive to all but a select few works. There is not even any guarantee that the appearance of a star author on television will attract callers in quantities that make the 900 gimmick a potential gold mine. One reason is that the kind of people who watch television may not be the kind who buy books; or those who read books may not be the type who respond to an invitation to phone their favorite author. In limited tests of the concept, a book that attracted tens of thousands of callers was one purporting that Elvis Presley is still alive and in communication with certain people. I wonder whether even a bestselling novelist could draw that kind of response.

And what about visionaries like Neil Schulman? Schulman's arguments about the inadequacies of present-day publishing are indisputable. Publishing is in trouble, perhaps fatally so. The technology for supplanting traditional publishing is certainly at hand. There is no reason why a completely electronic approach might not signal the start of a revolution in reading habits. But I do wonder about reading habits.

Maybe it's because I grew up in a world of books written on typewriters, printed in hot type by the descendants of Gutenberg, and read in bound sheets of paper distributed in bookstores. But I do seriously question why anybody would read a work of literature on a PC monitor when instead, she could curl up in her favorite chair with a bowl full of munchies and read a traditional book the good old-fashioned way. Or why one would go to the trouble of having a book reconstituted on his PC printer when he can acquire that same book in a store. The answer may be the handheld electronic "reader," but the technology for it simply isn't there yet. And when I asked Schulman—just out of curiosity, mind you—about the place of literary agents in this brave new world of his, he suggested that we might earn our livings helping our clients package their work for electronic transmission.

Humph!

■

Systems

T HAT IT IS MORE OF AN ART THAN A science is one of publishing's greatest glories, but it is also one of its most obstinate liabilities. The decision to acquire a book is drawn from such intangible values as taste, instinct, and passion. Yet these qualities may stand squarely in opposition to many relentless business realities. The tension between these values is as ancient as art itself and will never be satisfactorily resolved. But that is no reason why publishers should not strive to research such factors as distribution patterns, consumer habits, marketing efficiency, and return on investment, and to apply their findings to the formulation of sound business judgements.

Until recently, the state of market research in publishing was appallingly primitive. But the advent of giant bookstore chains like Barnes & Noble and Waldenbooks and wholesalers like Ingram and Baker & Taylor has made accurate statistical reporting imperative. And, happily, the development of sophisticated computers has given the managers of those and other publishing-related firms the capability to gather, analyze, and apply great quantities of statistical information toward the task of systematizing the publishing, book distribution, and bookselling industries.

Those of us, such as writers, agents, and consumers, who are not directly involved in those fields, may have only the dimmest idea of just how formidable that task is. Indeed, I would guess that most of the people who *are* directly involved do not appreciate how tremendous the challenge is, owing to the narrow focus of their daily jobs. The goal of setting uniform standards for such mundane activities as the design of book order forms, shipping labels, and invoices is equivalent in complexity and difficulty to the adoption of a single currency by the original American colonies. Yet failure to design such forms and get them accepted on an industry-wide basis has been a major cause of inefficiency and financial loss to publishers and booksellers. And that, in turn, translates into the kinds of disappointment with which authors are only too familiar.

Out of efforts to develop standard systems in these mundane but critical activities, the Book Industry Systems Advisory Committee (BISAC), was created. BISAC is a confederation of committees dedicated to improving publishing-industry efficiency in such areas as promoting the use of the International Standard Book Number (ISBN), developing computer-to-computer formats, and creating a universal method for placing and electronically scanning bar codes on books.

I was introduced to BISAC after accepting an invitation to join the organization's committee on royalty statements. That committee, consisting of publishers, literary agents, royalty managers, and computer systems specialists, was in the process of trying to formulate a standard royalty statement format that could be adopted by all publishers. It did not take long for me to realize that the ostensibly simple job of defining terms, organizing them in a sensible fashion, arranging them on a page for maximum comprehensibility, and creating computerized "fields" for translating information into computer-readable format, is actually fiendishly difficult, even without the complications of negotiating which information is acceptable to all interest groups. It was a humbling experience.

As any systems manager will tell you, the hardest part of the job is thinking. The members of BISAC are thinkers, and after hearing a presentation by its then-chairman, Mark Lilien, at an agents' meeting, I interviewed him to hear his observations about a variety of industry problems. He illuminated them brilliantly, and convinced me how imperative it is that we on the seller's side of the table understand what the people on the buyer's side are trying to accomplish.

Although (as we shall soon see) many publishing-industry problems call for vast and highly complex applications of computer programming genius, others, such as what to say on a shipping label and where to place that label on a box of books, are so simple that I'm willing to wager that you have never thought about them. But because until recently nobody else had, either, publishers and booksellers have suffered untold waste and lost profits.

Take a packing list. Every carton of books must contain one so that the bookstore employee opening the box may verify the order. It would seem as plain as day that the most desirable way to list the books in the box is alphabetically by title. But many publishers print their packing lists in random sequence. The reason is that the "pickers and packers," the warehouse employees who fulfill bookstore orders, do not usually select titles in alphabetical order, and do not list them alphabetically when they fill out their packing list. That may be all well and good for the pickers and packers, but it costs substantially extra time for workers at the bookstore to unload those cartons and check their contents against the packing list.

"Everyone in the store knows which publishers make their cartons easy to unpack and which ones make it hard," said Lilien. "Which ones do you think they are going to unpack first?" Yet he estimated that, amazingly, half the publishers in the business do not trouble to organize their packing lists alphabetically!

At the other end of the spectrum in complexity is the effort to place machine-readable bar codes on the covers of books to facilitate such processes as tallying sales, taking inventory, and processing returns. It should be obvious that the better a publisher's systems for accomplishing those tasks, the more effectively and profitably its business will be run. But here again, many publishers were slow to adopt the idea.

The notion of putting bar codes on books arose out of efforts by publishing-industry managers to utilize the computerized data-processing hardware that was emerging in the late 1970s and early 1980s to replenish book inventories automatically. The key was to find a way to track sales not merely by class but by item. The ISBN—that number you see on the copyright page of most books published today—was created to achieve that end. Yet in 1979, when Lilien took a job at Waldenbooks, many major publishers had not adopted ISBNs, and others employed numbering systems that were not compatible with those of bookstores. The bookstores themselves were groping for their own computerized ordering and inventory systems. One scheme seriously considered was a cash register with a key for each publisher: when a clerk rang up a sale of a Putnam book, he would press the Putnam key on the cash register in order to access Putnam's system of keeping track of books; when he pressed the Pocket Books key, he would access the Pocket Books system, etc.

Lilien was part of a team that attempted to raze this Tower of Babel. The idea was to create a uniform and universal means for stores and wholesalers to match orders to inventory, then communicate this information to central headquarters and to publishers. By the time this system was developed, Waldenbooks had become a significant force and was able to force publishers to use ISBNs if they wanted to do business with the chain. As publishers replaced aging computer systems with new ones, they were careful to buy hardware and software compatible with the needs of the chains.

Adoption of the ISBN book-numbering system was an important breakthrough for the industry. Among the benefits of using the ISBN is enhanced order processing, fulfillment accuracy, verification of orders, invoice reconciliation, referencing of inquiries, and proper crediting of returns.

The identification of individual books at the point of purchase, however, was still hampering the efficiency with which bookstore sales were recorded. But the emerging technology of machine-readable bar codes printed on the outside of products, which grocery and beauty product manufacturers and store chains were starting to employ, offered publishers a solution.

Most trade book publishers have adopted it, but not without tremendous growing pains. A random glance at a BISAC handbook called *Machine-Readable Coding Guidelines for the U.S. Book Industry* will give you an idea why publishers can't simply snap their fingers and change their system overnight:

> Size of OCR-A characters: The ISBN must be printed in OCR-A at 10 characters per inch. The preferred location of the ISBN/OCR-A is above the EAN bar code symbol. It may also be printed below the EAN bar code. Including all letters, numbers, spaces and hyphens the ISBN consists of 18 characters. At 10 characters per inch, the length is 1.8". An additional .1" clear area is required to the left and right for a total of 2". There must also be a space, or clear area, of .165" above and below the OCR-A characters. The total area that must be allowed for the ISBN printed in OCR-A, therefore, is approximately .435" high by 2.0" wide.

These terms are precise so that many different scanners will be able to read the bars accurately.

Even as the industry started to resolve the technical problems, others arose. Most notable was the fact that Europeans developed their own variation on the bar code—the European Article Number (EAN)—that was just different enough to make it incompatible with our Universal Product Code (UPC). This situation is analogous to the difference between the British and metric numerical systems. Although some solutions have been cobbled together as the publishing industry becomes more and more multinational, this disharmony may be a significant stumbling block to efficient marketing of American books overseas, and vice versa.

If the publishing industry adopted even half of BISAC's systems applications, it would have a fighting chance of entering the twentieth century.

Just in time for the twenty-first.

■

Understanding Authors

15

Endangered Species

WE OFTEN REFER TO THE PUBLISH-
ing world as an environment, and recently, as I discussed the state of
the industry with a colleague, I realized how apt the metaphor is. Why
is it, I asked, that some types of literature flourish while others fade
or perish? The answer seems to be that the healthiest genres spring
out of the richest and least-spoiled breeding grounds.

Breeding grounds are not particularly glamorous places: marshy
wetlands, dank rain forests, remote and dusty plains. Yet they produce
some of the most vigorous and beautiful of earth's species. By the
same token, the places where literature is incubated are often dark,
humble, and homely, far from the chic world of blockbusters and
spectacular seven-figure publishing deals. And most authors who
achieve stardom do not spring there fully formed; they emerge only
after a long, slow, and often painful gestation in that netherworld of
penny-a-word pulps, esoteric magazines, or even pornography.

I entered the publishing field at a time when there were still many
fecund habitats for authors to develop. By far, the most important of
these was the magazine field. Countless publications, ranging from

avant-garde to highbrow to slick to pulpy, published fiction of every kind. Agents did not turn their noses up at short stories as most of them do today, and although commissions on them seldom made up a large part of an agent's income, they did make an agreeable contribution to the rent. There were ten or fifteen markets or more for any story taken on by an agent, so if you couldn't place it for big money with the *Saturday Evening Post* or *Good Housekeeping,* you could hope to sell it eventually to the *Detroit Athletic Club News* or *Chatelaine* for $250 or $500. Western, mystery, adventure, horror, science fiction, confession, romance, and other genre magazines abounded, offering writers a plethora of outlets for their budding talents. More sophisticated, "slick" magazines such as the *Saturday Evening Post, Look, Redbook,* and *McCall's* devoted substantial space to fiction for men, women, and the general reader, and these publications commonly serialized novels. Somewhat elevated ones like the *New Yorker* and *Harper's* provided a haven to authors with literary ambitions, and there was an abundance of experimental and "little" magazines that could afford to pay their contributors only with subscriptions. Yet, a host of splendid authors apprenticed in such magazines, and the demise of those publications did incalculable damage to the development of new talent in subsequent years.

Another fertile hatchery for authors was paperback originals. In the 1950s and 1960s, this was largely a male phenomenon, and it was a booming one. The markets for western, crime, science fiction, war, and action-adventure paperbacks were accessible to any starting writer with talent, persistence, and fast fingers. The rates paid for this material put a premium on speed and the skill to turn out publishable copy in a single draft.

One genre in particular could be likened to a kind of salmon spawning ground, and that was soft pornography or, as it was called then, the sex novel. Sex novels were designed to string together the maximum number of sex scenes on the skimpiest thread of a story. Owing to obscenity laws that still carried some weight at that time, sex novels gingerly treaded a euphemism-strewn path between the Scylla of clinical anatomical terms and the Charybdis of vulgar ones.

At its peak in the early 1960s, the market for sex novels was insatiable, with some publishers turning out ten or twelve of them every month. The demand for writers was stupendous, and publishers generously rewarded any who could produce on a rigid assembly-line schedule. Some turned out three or four a month, and if a regular collapsed in harness leaving his publisher with an open slot that month, one of his colleagues might find himself called upon to turn a book out over a weekend.

You would probably be shocked to learn the names of some of today's leading novelists who got their start in sex books, producing dozens and even hundreds of them under pseudonyms before ever creating anything on which they wanted to put their own names. When they did at length turn their hands to other kinds of fiction, however, it was with fully realized capabilities, thanks to the opportunity afforded them by that very lowly genre, pornography.

The most important incubator of all is the literary first novel. Only a very short time ago, most trade publishers believed it was their responsibility if not their duty to reinvest some of the profit from successful books in the work of new authors. It was assumed that the initial output of those authors would lose money or, at best, break even before rewarding its patrons with a profit and eventually a bestseller. At the time I was learning the book trade some thirty-five years ago, that attitude was still an important factor in the decision-making process at most hardcover publishers. But that was a time when a publisher could break even on a five thousand-copy sale, and a burgeoning paperback reprint market could actually make a profitable venture out of what we today call, opprobriously, a midlist book.

Toward the end of the 1960s, a number of turbulent economic, cultural, and business trends placed these ecosystems in serious jeopardy. Many magazines got into trouble because both advertisers and subscribers were turning to television, and by the 1970s, the market had been decimated. Those publications that survived cut back radically on fiction, conceding the field to television sitcoms, western series, cop shows, and other types of programming that did not call for deeper investments of time and imagination than reading did. Whatever fiction magazines did still demand was from established, popular authors. New writers found themselves on the losing end of a struggle to recapture the kind of access they had enjoyed in the previous decades. A star system was beginning to emerge, and it was not to be limited to the magazine field.

Another major upheaval was a sort of ice age that descended on the male paperback market in the 1970s as female readers (and, some say, female editors) created a boom in mass-market paperback fiction for women that is still the dominant factor in original paperback publishing today. It started with gothic novels, which then gave way to formula historical and contemporary romances.

Although many male writers tried to shift their skills to these genres, and some succeeded, paperback editors usually insisted on women writers for women's fiction on the grounds that men weren't sufficiently sensitive to the romantic emotions that stirred in the female bosom. Thus did a new and vast breeding ground open up on the publishing landscape, creating conditions for women writers very similar to those of what might be called the golden age of male paperbacks: a seemingly infinite base of readers, an assembly-line approach to formula storytelling, accessibility of editors, and a seller's market for young talent.

The romance boom contained the seeds of its own recession as every paperback publisher jumped in and in due time glutted the market. Of late we have seen a softening of the women's paperback fiction category and the shutting down or curtailing of a number of struggling formula romance lines. The survivors of these cutbacks are a superb breed of women novelists who have advanced into leading positions in paperback, moved up to hardcover, or even broken out into serious mainstream endeavors. But with the tightening of the market comes a reduced demand for fresh female talent.

Once writers are driven from the market, it's very hard to get them back, and once again the comparison to a biosystem seems apposite, for when the population of certain species dwindles below a certain number, extinction becomes a foregone conclusion. It happened to an extent in the area of male-oriented fiction. During the 1970s, as women's fiction was rising to the fore, most of the male genres shrank to a fraction of what they once had been. Science fiction, mysteries, westerns, and male action-adventure did go on selling, but in sharply reduced quantities issued by secondary publishers like Pinnacle, Ace, Tower, and the then-fledgling Zebra. The larger and more powerful paperback houses, chasing after female readers, ignored the male. Except for a few stars like James Michener and John Jakes in historical, Stephen King in horror, Louis L'Amour in westerns, Robert Ludlum in international adventure, and a handful of science-fiction greats, it was hard to discover who spoke for, or to, male readers. A lot of male writers turned to nonfiction; a lot more went and did something else for a living.

Male fiction was regarded as a minor industry throughout much of the 1970s until some recessionary economic trends forced the big paperback houses to take another look at it. They realized that the market was vaster than they'd thought, and these companies thus began male fiction lines or acquired publishers of male fiction. As a result, there was an upswing in that market during the 1980s. But a toll had been exacted. During the darker age of the seventies, a combination of poor management and intensified competition drove out of business the weaker paperback houses which, schlocky as they might have been, provided a great market for new writers.

Hardest hit of all have been the breeding grounds for serious fiction. A series of recessionary cycles over the past few decades forced publishers to concentrate more and more on immediate, frontlist successes. Those houses unable to keep up have been forced to make one of a number of unpleasant choices: merge with other publishers, be acquired by nonpublishing conglomerates, or abandon their traditional commitment to quality in favor of the instant bestseller. Whichever they chose, it meant the rejection of a fundamental principle, namely, that talent requires time to mature.

The rise to dominance of paperback publishers exacerbated the problem, because paperback is an even more frontlist kind of publishing than hardcover. Paperbacks that don't prove themselves in a few weeks are usually doomed; they seldom are afforded the luxury of remaining in a store for months, available to browsers, the way hardcovers are (or used to be). The establishment of all-powerful chain stores with their emphasis on fast-moving bestsellers, and the elimination of publishers' slush piles as a source of new talent, have dumped more and more landfill into the breeding grounds. As we've seen, a great deal of the responsibility for discovering and nurturing new authors has fallen on the literary agents, but agents are not in a position to support authors with money, nor does their enthusiasm raise their clients' public recognition by one iota. All that agents can do is get an author's work onto an editor's desk; from that point on, the manuscript is at the mercy of a process that is essentially hostile to unperfected talent.

When we survey the current publishing scene, we see that the healthiest markets are those that continue to tap the wellsprings of new talent, much the way that successful major-league baseball teams draw from a deep farm system to replace aging stars. Science fiction, for example, thrives—and will continue to thrive—because of the abundance of magazines, the accessibility of editors, the frequent conventions around the country giving hopeful young authors exposure to their literary heroes and heroines, and slush piles that are still actively combed by editors for interesting work. Male action-adventure, romance, and westerns still have something of a support system, even though it is no longer what it used to be. In the area of serious literature, the *New Yorker* is far and away the most significant incubator for exciting talent, which is why the change in its editorial management sent such terrific tremors through the world of letters. The *New Yorker* is a landmark: its integrity must be preserved at any cost.

Several years ago, it was announced that a takeover war was in progress for the assets of Harper and Row, a war that eventually was won by Australian media baron Rupert Murdoch, who renamed it HarperCollins. The reason that would-be acquirers gave for coveting Harper was its rich backlist. A good backlist is a tremendous asset, as it generates steady income for a publisher without intensive investment of capital. But when you think about it, what is a backlist but a file drawer full of old contracts? Or, if we extend the metaphor of the environment one last time, we realize that a backlist is a sort of museum of natural history, depicting the kind of world we had when the breeding grounds were turbulent with life. If we do not find ways to generate tomorrow's backlist, to reopen or restock the breeding grounds, we may well awaken one day to the literary equivalent of a silent spring.

■

What's in a (Big) Name?

BEHOLD THE TWO BOOKS I PLACE before you. Both are thrillers by authors whose names are unfamiliar to you. But attached to the one on your left is an endorsement by one of today's bestselling thriller writers. The other has no such recommendation. Which will you be inclined to purchase and read?

The obvious answer to that question formed the eye of a tempest that recently swept through the publishing industry, leaving in its path a shattered deal, damaged credibility, and a dazed author and his agent wandering through the rubble seeking something to salvage. The only good to come out of this event is the possibility that the rest of us may learn something from it.

We take for granted that a plug from a star can give an enormous boost to an obscure author or an undistinguished (or even distinguished) book. That is why publishers go to considerable lengths to solicit quotes—commonly called "blurbs" in the publishing industry—by big-name authors for books they are soon to publish. "When 55,000 books are published each year, you are desperate for ways to distinguish your books from everybody else's," Paul Gottlieb, president of

Harry N. Abrams Inc. told *New York Times* then–media reporter Edwin McDowell. "The right person writing a blurb for the right audience can sometimes make a tremendous difference in sales."

What it was that inspired Peter Lampack, a leading literary agent, to put blurbs on an *unsold* manuscript, I do not know. But when I read in the newspaper that he had used the ploy to garner over $900,000 in an auction for a first novel, I could have kicked myself for not having thought of it first.

Lampack's strategy was simple but inspired. If he used the blurbs to sell the book to publishers, he would certainly arouse far more interest in the book than in a book supported only by his own enthusiasm. Because enthusiasm is as commonplace among agents as it is among mothers, it is subject to heavy discounting by skeptical publishers. If, however, an author of world-class reputation offers an enthusiastic quote, it all but guarantees that publishers will highly prize the work to which it's attached.

There are two important reasons why a plug from a star would give a big boost to an unsold book by an unknown author. The first is that it validates the book's quality for editors. Given the cost of publishing and promoting first novels, editors today are extremely nervous about committing their companies to investing hundreds of thousands or even millions or dollars for them. Not a few would rather pass up a good first book than overpay for it, for many an editorial head has been impaled on the pikestaff of poor judgment. If an author who is a proven moneymaker raves about that book, however—particularly an author seldom given to promoting the work of others—much of the uncertainty about its quality is taken out of the editor's hands. And so is the responsibility, thus freeing the editor to spend the company's money with confidence.

The other reason why an enthusiastic blurb by a star author is of such inestimable value is that it also validates the book for the consumer. As the average list price of a novel approaches, at this writing, $30 in hardcover and $7 in mass-market paperback, bookstore customers have become more discriminating than ever about what they plunk their money down for. It is likely that they will be inclined to pay that kind of money only for a proven commodity: a book by a brand-name author. If, however, a brand-name author declares adoration for an unheard-of book, and permits a publisher to feature his statement on cover and advertising copy, the publicity value of that plug will overcome consumer reluctance. After all, the next best thing to a book by your favorite bestselling author is a book that your favorite bestselling author loves and recommends. The late publisher Donald Fine stated in McDowell's *Times* article that "there's a presumption among marketing people that blurbs are especially important for the sales reps and booksellers." Fine cited the time when he asked John D. MacDonald to read galleys of a book by Elmore Leonard, who was at that time considered a midlist mystery writer. MacDonald called Fine and exclaimed, "Who is that guy? He's terrific." Fine asked MacDonald if he could use those very words in advertising for Elmore's books, and the rest is history.

Understanding these psychological principles so well, agent Lampack must have jumped for joy when Derek V. Goodwin, pseud-onymous author of a first novel entitled *Just Killing Time,* furnished him with blurbs by two of today's leading thriller authors, John Le Carré and Joseph Wambaugh. Lampack loved Goodwin's novel, and successfully solicited a quote from a famous client of his own, Clive Cussler. Thus armed with three dynamite blurbs, Lampack put *Just Killing Time* up for auction, and when the dust settled, Simon & Schuster walked off with the book with a high bid of $920,000.

I had scarcely had time to compose a congratulatory letter to Lampack when the newspapers announced that both Le Carré and Wambaugh had repudiated the blurbs attributed to them, Le Carré characterizing the one written over his name as "straight fraud." After an agonizing week, Simon & Schuster withdrew its offer. "We must be able to rely on the validity of what is submitted to us," stated the president of Simon & Schuster's trade division. The author claimed that he was "completely duped" by whoever it was that had issued the phony blurbs.

My heart went out to my colleague, a first-class agent and a gentleman of the highest character, and I waited breathlessly to see who, if anyone, would come forward to claim the orphaned book. During the month or so it took for that question to be answered, the debacle set off a fascinating debate: How much was Goodwin's book worth without the quotes? As I listened to the arguments, I thought of the ancient dispute as to whether a tree that falls in a forest makes a sound if no one is present to hear it. Goodwin's book after the deal fell through was the same one that existed before. The only difference was, two of the three star blurbs had been dropped. So had the price. Simon & Schuster's winning bid had been withdrawn, and it didn't seem likely that the runner-up in the auction, Bantam with $850,000, would stand by its offer. How much was Goodwin's book worth stripped of its glamorous advocates? Even more interesting to me was: How much were the big-name author blurbs worth? I said above that they were of inestimable value, but if you look at it in a certain way, you will realize they can indeed be estimated.

As it turned out, Lampack was able to resell Goodwin's book for approximately a $500,000 advance to Dutton Press/New American Library, a division of the Penguin organization and an underbidder in the original auction. Can it not be argued that the blurbs by Le Carré and Wambaugh were therefore worth $420,000, the difference between what Simon & Schuster would have paid for the book with blurbs and what the new publisher was willing to pay without them? That would mean that Le Carré's and Wambaugh's blurbs could each be valued at $210,000.

It would not surprise me to learn that it had crossed the minds of these distinguished authors, or the minds of their distinguished agents, that there is big money to be earned in selling their endorsements. Movie stars and other celebrities get big bucks for endorsing all sorts of products. Why shouldn't star authors get them for plugging books? Requests for blurbs are an imposition on an author's time, and for a big-name author, time is not just money—it's a lot of money. On those grounds alone, then, it can be argued that an author ought to be compensated. But more importantly, there is the obvious fact that the author's name helps to sell the merchandise. Robert Ludlum and

Stephen King were paid handsomely to star in American Express card commercials; why would they be out of line demanding money to do a "commercial" for someone else's book?

Our instincts rebel against the notion because it seems dishonest—and our instincts are correct. Unlike commercials undertaken for pay, the author who writes a blurb is assumed to genuinely like the product he or she is promoting. There is thus an aura of sincerity about blurbs that would be fatally tarnished if they were written for pay. Of course, one could be cynical about that sincerity, as it often appears that the blurbing industry operates under the motto, "One hand washes the other." *Spy* magazine carried a feature called "Logrolling in Our Time," which cited the suspicious frequency with which an author who plugs another's book finds his or her own book praised in return by the pluggee of the first part. In one issue, for instance, after George F. Will is quoted as calling Henry Kissinger's *The White House Years* "an elegant literary achievement," Kissinger is quoted as calling Will's *The Pursuit of Virtue and Other Tory Notions* "a delight." Similarly, Barbara Ehrenreich and John Kenneth Galbraith, Richard Ford and Joyce Carol Oates, and Diane Johnson and Francine Prose are shown to be mutual admirers of each other's books.

Such possible abuses notwithstanding, the point is that blurbs are traditionally undertaken as favors, and are therefore a form of barter. And though publishers and agents who request them from their authors don't usually offer specific inducements, the good will generated by a cooperative author inevitably pays off down the road in one tangible way or another. As an editor once said to me, "It's good business to caress the hand that feeds you."

But good will is a fragile value and the lofty tradition of exchanging favors cannot always be counted on to prevail over the temptations of hard cash. A day may well come when a famous writer will demand a big fee for endorsing someone's book, and a publisher will pay it. Anyone naïve enough to think it can't happen has never attended a baseball card convention, where star ballplayers who used to autograph memorabilia out of the goodness of their hearts now charge hefty fees for their appearances and signatures. It's not hard to imagine the lyrics of Simon & Garfunkel's famous song being altered to, "Where have you gone, Ernest Hemingway?"

The fact is that just as light is bent by the gravitational pull of celestial stars, our ethics seem to get a little bent by the attraction of human stars. Take for instance what might be termed the "Dead Author's Society," wherein publishers go on issuing works by authors long in their graves. The bylines of such illustrious writers as V. C. Andrews and Cynthia Freeman continue to appear on books long after the passage of their namesakes into the place from which there is no returning. You would be surprised how many fans are under the impression that the authors are still alive, an impression the publishers have not gone out of their way to correct. Is this ethical?

I don't particularly deplore the practice, as I'm not sure I see that much difference between books packaged by dead authors and those packaged by living ones—and living ones do it all the time. Whether the spurious books are as good as those created by the original authors is another question, but if most fans never notice the difference, the issue of quality is pretty much beside the point.

In England, it's considered not just unethical but downright illegal for a publisher to issue a book with the byline of a deceased author. Of course, the British have always been a bit dotty about their dead big-name authors. Would you believe they actually enshrine some of them in their cathedrals?

■

Shared Worlds

SOME TIME AGO, THE COMMUNITY for Creative Non-Violence, an advocacy group for the homeless, commissioned a Baltimore sculptor, James Earl Reid, to create a sculpture. In due time, his skilled hands produced a piece called *Third World America,* celebrating the dignity and suffering of homeless people. It was a work that both the advocacy group and the sculptor could be proud of, and they were. But then, as both began making plans to take it on tour, a question arose that nobody had bothered to explore in any depth: Who owns *Third World America?* The Community for Creative Non-Violence claimed the sculpture was a "work made for hire." Not only had the group hired the sculptor, but had also imparted to him its vision of what the piece should look like, and had even given him much input on details. Be that as it may, claimed Reid, he was the sole creator of the work and he should retain the copyright.

The dispute triggered a legal battle culminating in a Supreme Court decision that has important implications for writers. For, if you substitute "publisher" or "packager" for the group that hired Reid, "writer" for "sculptor," and "book" for "sculpture," you have a perfectly analogous relationship to one quite commonly found on the publishing scene. Under the "work-for-hire" provision of the Copyright Act of 1976, publishers, packagers, magazines, newspapers, and other persons or businesses may copyright in their own names works that they conceive and"farm out" to freelance writers. Like the Committee for Creative Non-Violence, these parties originate the writing projects, furnish writers with detailed specifications, and offer writers abundant editorial guidance. Are they not, then, entitled to claim ownership of copyright to those works? Are they not entitled to exploit those works in whatever way they wish, with no further obligation to the writers?

According to the Supreme Court, which ruled on the dispute on June 5, 1989, the answer is no. The decision was unanimous.

The court's ruling hinged not so much on the amount of time, effort, thought, vision, and money the advocacy group had invested in the sculpture, but rather on whether or not the artist could justly be described as an employee of the group that hired him. It seems that when Congress created the revised copyright law, it left the definition of work for hire somewhat ambiguous, describing it as "a work prepared by an employee within the scope of his or her employment." Had the sculptor gone to work on salary for a company that mass-produced plastic Buddhas, he would obviously have no claim to the product he helped to manufacture. But Reid's relationship to the organization that commissioned his sculpture was nowhere so simple, and his attorneys attacked the vagueness of the terms "employee" and "scope of employment."

"Under the broadest alternative," wrote Linda Greenhouse of the *New York Times,* "a freelance artist was an 'employee,' and therefore forfeited the right to copyright his or her work whenever the party commissioning the work, like a magazine publisher, retained the right to 'control' the final product." Greenhouse reported that a group of major publishers had filed a brief as friends of the Court, supporting this definition. That should come as no surprise, considering how much is at stake for them. Until the sculpture decision, most freelance work was considered work-for-hire. The result of the Supreme Court's decision, however, is that freelance writers and artists may enjoy, to a far greater extent than before, the benefits of copyright to the work they produce for others. "The fee that these businesses pay to a freelance artist will be a fee for one-time use of the work and not, as has been common practice, for the right to reprint and reuse the material without further compensation," stated Greenhouse.

Reid, the Court asserted, is an independent contractor and not an employee, and therefore his sculpture was not a "work made for hire." Because of the ambiguity of the origins of the work, however, the Court sent the case back to a lower court to consider whether the sculpture might fall into yet another category of copyright law, a joint work to which the copyright was owned by both claimants coequally.

It's interesting that this development comes at a time when the question of "moral rights" has begun to raise writers' consciousness about the status of freelance work they perform for outside contractors. I have speculated on the changes in the relationship between contractors and freelancers if American courts should adopt the principle that authors and artists are entitled to moral rights protection of their creations even though they have sold their copyrights to other parties. The Supreme Court's decision on Reid's sculpture is not a moral rights one, but it does give artists and writers a beachhead to wage further battles to protect work that they have sold—or thought they had sold—outright.

What seems to have been glossed over in the press's coverage of the sculpture battle is the extent of the contract between the commissioning party and the sculptor or, indeed, whether there was a written agreement at all. The relationship between the parties might not have stirred up such bitter conflict had they "perfected" it, to use a legal term, through a clearly worded contract in which the status of copyright ownership was spelled out. The deal between them, however, seems to have arisen in a spirit of good will and genuine compassion for the poor and homeless, but very little else in terms of a tightly structured contract. What seems to be implied in the Supreme Court's decision is, If you don't want any misunderstandings about ownership of copyright, you'd better write a good contract.

There are many cautionary lessons in this legal case that should be of particular interest to writers. For instance, inadequate grasp of the legal implications of arrangements writers make with book packagers has caused a great deal of grief for many authors. Book packagers copyright in their own name the projects they create, and writers they hire to develop those projects are denied proprietary interest in the work they perform for packagers. Packagers, in other words, are in a position analogous to that of the Community for Creative Non-Violence, the outfit that engaged the sculptor and subsequently claimed copyright ownership of the piece he did for them. "Packager" is, for some writers, a loaded term, connoting exploitation. I have stated elsewhere that I don't think there is anything inherently wrong with book packagers, but writers entering into contracts with them should do so with their eyes open and be aware of the nature of their relationship to packagers. There are fair packagers, not-so-fair packagers, and wicked packagers, but central to their activities is the copyrighting of literary creations in their own name. This process can be perceived as unfair if one party feels that he or she has been taken advantage of by the other.

Even harder for many writers to grasp are the implications of so-called shared-world series or anthologies. Shared worlds are generated out of popular books or series. The authors of these works, and their publishers, exploit the popularity of the books' characters by licensing or commissioning other authors to write new works featuring those characters and the world they live in. An example of this is the series of anthologies created in Andre Norton's Witch World. These collections of stories by other authors extend and elaborate on the fantasy world originally created in a series of books by Norton. Shared worlds, though we don't always think of them that way, may be found in categories outside of science fiction and fantasy. In the male action-adventure genre, for example, authors created new stories for the world of The Executioner originally created by Don Pendleton. Hardy Boys and Nancy Drew novels were produced by writers for hire long after the deaths of the authors who created these characters. The sequel to *Gone with the Wind,* when you strip away all the hype, was essentially a shared-world novel.

A tremendous amount of confusion exists about shared worlds, and misunderstandings about the relationship between creator and sharers have caused strain and even enmity among formerly warm friends and colleagues when arguments over money, byline credits, and copyright ownership developed. Perhaps many of these problems would take a proper perspective if all parties realized a fundamental truth about shared worlds: the moment an author attempts to share his world with other authors, he becomes, in effect, a packager.

At the heart of most such grievances is that sudden change in the way sharers and "sharees" relate to each other. Writers who, up to then, were on what might be called a communistic parity with other writer comrades, suddenly become capitalists, and they don't always handle their new role very well. The tasks of apportioning money and credits produce conflicting feelings in authors who for so long have themselves struggled in the position of the exploited. "I felt," one writer told me, "like an assembly-line worker who had suddenly been made foreman. In negotiating contracts with authors sharing my world with me, I had to pull rank on some of my former co-workers, and none of us was happy about it."

Thanks to the Supreme Court's ruling, conflicts over money and credits may not be the only sources of contention between the participants in shared-world deals. Serious questions of ownership may be raised by contributors of material to shared-world series or anthologies. If you write a sequel or prequel to somebody else's novel, are you entitled to claim ownership, or co-ownership, of your contribution? Unless you clearly waived such a claim when you signed an agreement with the original author, the answer may well be debatable.

If you're not sure what's at stake, consider the lawsuit brought by Lynn Thomson, a dramaturg (a sort of script doctor for plays), against the estate of Jonathan Larson, author of the runaway Broadway hit musical, *Rent*. Before his tragic death, Larson had asked Thomson's advice on aspects of the show's script. Thomson subsequently claimed a co-authorship role entitling her to a share of the millions the Larson estate has earned, and will earn. In July 1997, a federal trial judge found that she was not a "joint author" under the U.S. Copyright Act, because she had not, in his opinion, contributed copyrightable material to the work, and because there was no evidence that she and Larson intended to be joint authors. Evidence—as in *contract*. The case is on appeal as of this writing, but whichever way it's decided, one could not ask for a more graphic illustration of the need to spell out the copyright implications of any arrangement, however casual, that authors make with those advising them on their texts.

Another ongoing lawsuit (at the time of this writing) concerns Fay Vincent, former commissioner of Major League Baseball. He was under contract to write his autobiography with a co-author, but presently thought better of publishing some revelations and decided to cancel the contract. His collaborator, however, claimed equal ownership of the manuscript under U.S. copyright law, meaning he has as much right as Vincent to bring out the memoir. The co-author's relationship to Vincent was apparently not writer-for-hire, but rather collaborator, and he does have a point. Another case of: Think before you share.

Up to now, too many authors have relied on the Golden Rule in reaching understandings with fellow authors about exploiting each other's worlds. If legal developments continue on the path they currently are following, it will be advisable to trade in the Golden Rule for an airtight contract.

■

Down on the Levy

AS IF IT WEREN'T HARD ENOUGH for writers to make a living, another menace has been growing, subtly and insidiously, to rob them of the fruits of their labors. I'm referring to the taxes imposed on money paid to American authors by foreign publishers. The time has come to blow the whistle on foreign governments that are taking shameless advantage of our authors to the tune of 10, 20, or 30 percent, or more, of the money to which they are entitled. And lest American publishers feel that this isn't their problem, let me stress at the outset that they are every bit as much victims as are the authors, for the very same imposts laid on American authors are exacted on money going to American publishers.

The problem has its origins in the reciprocal arrangements most western nations have concerning the imposition of income taxes. To put it simply, if you are an American citizen or company paying U.S. income taxes, then you are not required to pay taxes to a foreign government on income you earn from the licensing of foreign rights to your literary properties. Until not long ago, many foreign governments did not even bother to ascertain whether the American authors receiving money from publishers in those countries were American citizens. Those that did try to verify citizenship required a minimum of paperwork, usually the signing of an affidavit before a notary or a declaration by the Internal Revenue Service (IRS) that the author was a tax-paying U.S. citizen or resident.

In the last few years, however, a number of foreign governments have come to view book deals as a potentially lucrative source of revenue, and have levied taxes on money going to American authors and publishers that are not recoverable. And those governments that do eventually release or refund withheld taxes have made the requirements so complex and time consuming that months, and sometimes a year or more, may pass before the author gets relief.

I am not talking about countries like China or Bulgaria or Hungary where a certain degree of civil service obstructionism is to be expected. I'm talking about such countries as France, Germany, and Spain. I'm talking in particular about England, which has not given Americans tax headaches of this size since the Stamp Act of 1765.

With the help of my agency's subsidiary rights director, Amy Meo, I've assembled a country-by-country rundown of the tax situation as it affects American authors and publishers.

- GERMANY Although the German government has not yet gotten tough about taxes, an author is strongly advised to fill out a form furnishing their Social Security number and the address of their local IRS office. Payments owing to American authors could be held up if this information is not provided. In addition, authors must obtain a Form 6166 from the IRS, certifying that they filed a tax return in the prior year.
- SPAIN Spanish tax exemption must be obtained at least once a year. Authors must obtain Form 6166 from the IRS, which they then file with their Spanish publisher. However, if an author is represented by an agent, the agent may include the author under the umbrella of corporate filings for all the agency's clients. Failure to file results in a 20 percent tax on the author's money.
- FRANCE American authors and publishers must file Form 6166 to avoid paying a 33 percent tax on advances and royalties paid

on licenses of literary material to French publishers. As with Spain, French authorities require you to refile for exemption every year.

- ITALY Italy's setup is similar to that of France, except that the tax is currently 22.5 percent if you don't file for exemption, and 5 percent even if you do. Again, authors anticipating revenue in any given year must file an exemption form even though they originally filed one for that literary property the year before, or two or three or four years ago.

- JAPAN The Japanese impose a 20 percent tax on money earmarked for American authors and publishers, but Japanese publishers apparently file a document that automatically cuts the 20 percent tax in half. Nevertheless, a 10 percent tax is imposed on money going to American authors and publishers, and it is not refundable.

- ENGLAND It may come as a surprise to readers familiar with the dreadful bureaucracies of some European and Asian nations, but as of this writing, the prize for red tape unquestionably goes to the English government. The procedure for exempting American payees from English tax has always been tedious, but recently the country's Inland Revenue Bureau added some wrinkles that lead one to wonder whether it is deliberately making it hard for authors to get their money, in order to earn for the Exchequer interest on withheld taxes. In order for agents to help clients avoid a 23 percent tax on money owed by a British publisher, we have to go through the following procedure:

1. As soon as we make a deal for the author, we fill out a British tax-exemption form detailing the names and addresses of the British publisher and agent, the date of the contract, the information about the advance and royalty rate. We then mail the form to the author.

2. The author fills in name and address and answers nine questions ascertaining citizenship, residency, travel history, business activities, etc., signs a declaration, and mails the form to a regional Internal Revenue Service center. The author must

follow this procedure for every British publisher to whom he or she sells a book. The exemption is good for five years.

3. At the IRS center, an official certifies that "the last United States tax return filed by the claimant was made as a citizen or resident of the United States." The IRS official is then supposed to mail the certified form to England's Inspector of Foreign Dividends (a branch of the Inland Revenue Bureau), and to send notification to the author that certification is on its way to England. Whether the certification is airmailed or sent in the cargo hold of a tramp steamer, I am not sure. Given the amount of time it takes for the Inspector of Foreign Dividends to process the certification, it really doesn't make that much difference.

4. When the Inspector of Foreign Dividends receives the certification from the IRS, it processes the form and issues the author or his or her British agent a tax-exemption number. If the Inspector receives your certification in the spring, the trees will probably be bare by the time you are notified that your tax exemption has come through. If your British publisher pays the advance after the tax-exemption number has been issued, you will not have any tax withheld from your advance. If, however, the tax exemption has not come through at the time the publisher pays the advance, the 23 percent tax must be withheld and remitted to the Inland Revenue Bureau. You must then fill out another form when your advance does finally arrive, petitioning the Inland Revenue people to release the tax to you.

At length—and I mean *length*—the Inland Revenue will release your money—in pounds sterling. This will require you to put the check (or, more accurately, cheque) through for collection at your American bank and wait several more months for the funds to clear, a process usually attended by an exorbitant charge for the conversion of foreign currency.

This, then, is what you have to go through with English taxes. It makes me wonder why we are exporting our technology, giving them our McDonald's franchises, and shielding them beneath our nuclear umbrella.

With up to one third of the sums owing to American authors and publishers being seized or held hostage to the vagaries of foreign bureaucracies, it is high time for all the organizations representing American authors, agents, and publishers to raise their voices in protest.

Either that or give Americans a voice in those foreign governments. It would do well for us to remind them that No Taxation without Representation is a cornerstone of American democracy. We fought a war over it. And we won.

■

Outrageous Fortune

I OFTEN PONDER THE ROLE PLAYED by luck in the fates of books and authors. Are some authors luckier than others? Are there lucky breaks for writers, the literary equivalent of the understudy who replaces a lead actor in a show and becomes a star overnight? Do we make our own luck? Can good luck be bought or manipulated? Can bad luck be avoided? Are some of us simply, to use the poignant Yiddish word, schlemazels, those hapless folks who always seem to be standing under the flowerpot when it falls from a windowsill?

Our natural egotism rejects the notion that our successes or failures are the products of random and indiscriminate accidents. This may be particularly true for writers, not (just) because they possess an excessive supply of egotism, but because as intellectuals it is their task to rationalize their world, and the only way to do that is to start with some assumptions about human beings' control over their destinies. What, after all, is fiction but the depiction of human heroes and heroines employing their wit, skill, strength, and other resources to defeat antagonists and overcome adversity? What would become of our fiction if the protagonists' achievements were portrayed as nothing more than lucky?

As we know, the road to publication is mined with perils. It takes intelligence, determination, and fortitude to avoid or conquer them. Yet, in my experience, there is no guarantee that these virtues will prevail in the writing game. Indeed, there's no guarantee that the most important asset of all, talent, will emerge victorious, at least not without a little assistance from good fortune. For while writing is certainly a solitary occupation, publishing is a social enterprise involving scores of critical processes performed by numerous individuals, many of whom possess considerably less enthusiasm for the product than the author does. And beyond the mechanics of publication and distribution are processes of a magnitude and complexity impossible to reckon, including trends and fads that are no more predictable than the course of a cyclone.

Any attempt to grasp this leaves us wondering how any books at all ever manage to succeed with so many hostile factors militating against them. Indeed, though I have handled many successful books in my career, I can recall only a handful that behaved in a way that might be described as an agent's dream, that is, were textbook case histories of books that performed precisely the way they were supposed to if everybody did his or her job. For me, the perfect publishing experience is a unicorn, glimpsed in my fantasies but never captured.

There was the Vietnam War novel that I sold to the perfect editor at the perfect publisher, which went on to do a great job of publication, eliciting dream reviews and sensational sales. At every step of the way I rubbed my eyes with astonishment and kept wondering when something would go wrong. Fortunately, it never did. The book went on to become not just a bestseller, but a backlist staple that continued to earn solid royalties year after year.

I am, of course, happy to take my share of the credit for the success of this book, and I'm sure that that success was created in some measure by my enthusiasm, commitment, and effort. But, looking back, I realize that Lady Luck influenced that book's destiny far more than I did, for there were numerous moments when disaster could have struck but was averted, as if the book were defended by an invisible shield. For example, some months before publication, the three principal editors who had acquired and sponsored the novel quit or were fired, leaving the book in danger of having no champion at the publisher to guide it through the hazards of publication. Providence intervened, however, in the form of a key executive in the sales department who happened to be a veteran of Vietnam and stepped into the role of protector. Similar threats arose to imperil the book after that, yet it seemed to be under a star. Perhaps the same star that brought it to me in the first place, for I have speculated on what fate might have befallen it had it been offered to an agent who didn't love it as much as I did, or if I had submitted it to a less suitable publisher.

In another instance, a writer submitted a police thriller to our agency. The format was awful: he had typed his book single-spaced on canary yellow paper, then bound the manuscript so tightly you needed a crowbar to read the left side of every page. In addition, the writer had not queried us before sending his book, but simply submitted his big fat manuscript unsolicited. The book seemed to be begging for rejection. But the first page or two arrested the attention of the assistant who took it out of its mailer, and he showed it to me. I was predisposed to dislike it, particularly the single-spaced aspect, for an agent's eyes are his most precious tool and this manuscript would have triggered a migraine headache by the third chapter. But I too liked the first few pages. "If he wants to retype the whole damn thing double-spaced, I'll look at it," I snapped at my young colleague. I figured it would be three months before I saw the book again, if ever. It showed up on my desk two days later. I hadn't reckoned on the formatting capabilities of what were at that time newfangled gadgets called word processors. It turned out to be a marvelous read, and I sold it for quite a lot of money to a hardcover publisher, which sold it for twice that much to a reprinter. Foreign and movie deals followed in quick order. But I wonder what would have happened if my assistant hadn't persisted. The book may well never have seen the light of day.

If a book is the bearer of bad karma, even the most hardworking author, enthusiastic agent, and committed publisher may not be able to overcome what appear to be the machinations of evil spirits. Editors leave their companies, abandoning books at critical moments; publishers are sold or acquired, playing havoc with books making their way toward the light of day; competitive books pop up out of nowhere to steal the limelight from what was expected to be a surefire bestseller; production snafus create fatal delays, putting books in stores too late to sell when they were intended to; trends veer off in unexpected directions, leaving great books stranded on the caprices of popular taste.

We are not talking about bad publishing, or wrong decision making, or poor judgment. We're simply talking about fate, the things that can happen to books when all of the gods watching over them happen to be named Murphy.

A few years ago my agency handled a business book by one of America's most prominent moguls. It had everything going for it and I'd have bet the store that nothing could stand in the way of this baby hitting the bestseller list and staying there a good long time. Another baron of industry had brought out a book of his own a short while before my guy's, however. That man's name was Lee Iacocca, and his autobiography was nothing short of the biggest hardcover bestseller in publishing history to that time, a book whose sales, heaven help the author, challenged those of the Bible itself. And although our book performed respectably by ordinary standards, it was utterly eclipsed by Iacocca's.

You might think that bad luck can be warded off by the expenditure of a lot of money, by researching the competition, by taking every precaution to produce the book competently, position it shrewdly, promote it vigorously, and sell it enthusiastically. It just isn't so. Fickle Fortune's finger taps any book, any author its whims designate. Even one superstar author, it was rumored, became upset when she learned her latest blockbuster was pitted in the same month against another author's latest blockbuster, threatening that guaranteed number one bestseller position she had come to assume was her right. And who can blame her for making that assumption, considering the millions spent on acquiring and publishing her books? Yet, all that money couldn't control another publisher's schedule.

I've had similarly sad experiences with a few books. A beauty book by a leading figure in the cosmetics world should have had it made, with a committed publisher, a strong advertising and promotion campaign, the whole bit. But it was published at the tail end of a beauty book trend in which the laurels had all been awarded to the likes of Jane Fonda, Victoria Principal, and Adrienne Arpel. The buyers were just not there, and there was nothing anybody could do about it. In another instance, a publisher paid a ton of money for a medical book we were handling. A little while later, that publisher acquired another author whose popular books on medical subjects almost invariably went to the top of the bestseller lists. There was clearly a conflict of interest here, and when it became obvious that my client's book was going to be on the losing end of that conflict, I protested and pulled his book from the publisher. It was clear that the publisher was prepared to sacrifice all that money paid to my client in order to land an even bigger author.

And I remember a show-business client of mine who had written a beautiful novel. After I sold it, the publisher invited him in to chat about promotion. At the meeting, the author boasted he could furnish plugs from just about any celebrity they could name. The promotion people's eyes lit up. "Great!" they gasped. And, true to his word, he brought in a sheaf of star endorsements an inch thick. There was scarcely enough room in the ads to fit them all.

And how did his book fare?

Don't ask.

It's one thing for a single book to flop because of bad luck. Most of us pick ourselves up, dismiss the experience philosophically, contemptuously, or humorously, and get on with our lives. It's quite another matter when one's entire career comes to grief, when unforeseen calamities befall book after book, crushing the author under the burden of misfortune. We know that there are winners and losers in the writing game—as there are in every other, but it is impossible to be philosophical or good humored when, over a stretch of time and a string of good books, everything goes wrong—and goes wrong consistently. I know of more than one author who can identify with the one who has had seven or eight books published and on not a single one did the editor who'd acquired it remain at the company long enough to see it published.

And there is more than one soul staggering around shell-shocked after seeing his first book crushed by a corporate takeover, his second sucked into the maelstrom of its publisher's bankruptcy, a third shut out of the stores in the Christmas sales season because a production snafu delayed publication by two months; and a fourth, fifth, and sixth orphaned after their editors quit their jobs or got the sack. Fires and floods in the warehouse, presidential assassinations, newspaper strikes—you name it, it's befallen these unfortunate souls.

Literary agents exist to even the odds against malevolent providence. We cannot, of course, prevent such calamities, but we may be able to help our clients avoid them, or rescue them before it's too late. If I've heard a rumor that a publisher may be up for sale, I am certainly not going to submit anything there until the situation stabilizes. And, on a more routine level, we try to locate the editor who will do best by a book, to push for promotional campaigns, to make sure our clients' books are scheduled for the most appropriate season, to reintroduce books to editors who have replaced those who originally acquired the properties. In short, we can maneuver our authors into the best possible positions to take advantage of good luck and evade bad.

We are certainly not deities, however, and we are still dependent to a good degree on luck. Years ago I launched an author's career when I sold her book to an editor who was so compatible with her that it seemed he had been put on earth specifically to minister to her work. One December day, just before the holidays, she visited my office and presented me with a bottle of champagne. "This," she declared, "is for your brilliance in selecting the perfect editor for me." Modestly, I lowered my eyes. How would she feel, I wondered, if she knew the truth: that on the day I'd sold her first novel, I had called six or eight editors I thought were more appropriate. They were all on vacation, ill, or too busy to come to the phone, and one was simply in the ladies' room. The "perfect" editor I had so presciently selected had actually been way down toward the bottom of my list! I decided not to tell my client. A magician never reveals his secrets, and besides, I like champagne.

I could tell countless more stories about agents who just happened to be in the right place at the right time. The point is simply that success isn't everything we crack it up to be. Good luck plays a tremendous part, and though the most successful businesspeople are those who are best prepared to deal with fortunate coincidences, and who place themselves in the best position for lucky breaks to happen to them, nobody has the advantage over anybody else in making luck happen.

But it's a strange thing about luck. The lucky look back and see one or two incredibly fortunate accidents, godsends as it were. The unlucky look back and see a conspiracy of evil forces that seemed to stalk them deliberately and maliciously. And perhaps that is how those who have lost in this nasty game may console themselves. There are so many good writers who have not made it, talented and industrious people whose careers don't deserve to perish, who have done everything necessary to win, yet still they fail. Perhaps, instead of blaming themselves or immolating themselves in guilt, they can hold their heads up and say, "I had some hard luck."

■

Green-Eyed Monsters

OVER THE YEARS THAT I'VE BEEN writing about the publishing scene, I've discussed many disturbing by-products of the consolidation of the industry. There is one, however, that I've been very reluctant to talk about because it cuts so very close to the anxieties that lurk in the darkest recesses of every author's heart. And that is the emotion of envy. It is as nasty and corrosive a passion as can be found among the seven deadly sins, and although it's impossible to demonstrate statistically, many editors and agents to whom I have spoken believe that it has been intensifying over the past few years. "Writers have always been a nervous lot," one editor said to me, "but lately it seems as if the pot is always seething." "They're angry all the time," another told me. "It's beginning to interfere with my effectiveness," an agent confided in me. He was referring to what he termed "mass hysteria among authors."

Authors are no different from anybody else in aspiring to fame, fortune, and status, and in suffering feelings of resentment, depression, and anger when their aspirations are frustrated. Are those feelings stronger and deeper today than before? I have the sense that they are. In fact, there are signs that author rage is becoming institutionalized in the form of unprecedented pressure on agents and publishers to match or exceed each record-breaking deal. In this sense, authors are contributing to the ever-accelerating cyclone that has already blown scores of publishers out of existence in the last decade or two, and that has driven a thousand writers out of the game for each one it has enriched.

I don't pretend to be exempt from this or the other deadly sins (I'm particularly big on gluttony), and as I'm right in the thick of things trying to secure those record-breaking deals for my own authors, I realize that I'm part of the problem. Still, I think the phenomenon of author envy is very much worth exploring, because it is so devastating to the peace of mind that authors must have in order to produce their best work, and because it creates unrealistic expectations that must, of necessity, lead to disappointment, dissatisfaction, and disillusionment.

What is envy? One dictionary defines it as ill will because of another's possessions or advantages. The dictionary distinguishes envy from jealousy, which is defined as fear, suspicion, or resentment of rivals, but for me the two terms might be used interchangeably. Peter Breggin, M.D., a psychiatrist and author, feels that jealousy is the more positive of the two emotions, because in wanting what somebody else has, you may be creatively inspired. Whereas envy is destructive in that you don't want somebody to have what he has. "Envy," he explains, "is debilitating in that it leaves you helpless and impotent." Whether or not you accept Breggin's distinctions, they focus on the core issue: invidious comparisons. Somebody is getting more money than you, more attention, bigger ads, better covers, and so on.

What makes me say that this kind of hostility is on the rise? Well, certain contributing factors are actually quantifiable. One is the refinement of bestseller lists, which are kept up-to-the-minute by computerized recordkeeping weekly systems. Unlike the *New York Times* or *Publishers Weekly* lists, the chain lists rank books on scales extending to as many as one hundred books, and *Publishers Weekly's* annual roundups list hundreds of bestsellers in descending order of sales. Genre publications have created their own bestseller lists in recent years, as well as review space devoted to science fiction, fantasy, horror, historicals, contemporary romance, and other category fiction. Also, genre fiction has begun to appear with growing frequency on the trade bestseller lists. Today's authors simply have many more opportunities than ever before to eat their hearts out.

Another principal factor is the shrinking of the publishing market-place, and this too can be proven statistically. Whereas there used to be plenty of publishers to go around, the consumption of publishing companies by other publishing companies has cut the number of viable trade markets by something on the order of 75 percent, leaving us with twelve or fifteen major houses orbited by countless small presses. An author surveying possible outlets for his or her work will simply find fewer than ever before. This narrowing of the funnel engenders tremendous emotional turbulence among authors, and sometimes a kind of combative competitiveness that is all but gladia-torial in nature. Norman Mailer has likened bestseller rivalry to boxing rankings. He once actually compared himself to a heavyweight champion defending his title, pugnaciously challenging all comers to knock him out of the ring.

Still another factor is increased publicity for bestsellers and big deals. The big publishers have large and well-heeled publicity depart-ments committed, as the phrase goes, to "moving books off the book page" and onto the front page or feature pages of newspapers and magazines, or into prime time television programs devoted to the world of entertainment.

The hyping of their books is certainly gratifying to authors, but there is definitely a downside. "Publishers are attempting to make midlist or genre authors into something they're not," a bookseller told a *Publishers Weekly* reporter for a year-end summary of books that had flopped that year. Another bookseller expressed alarm about the hype for big printings. "I look at the advertised 100,000 or 200,000 copies and wonder what publishers are thinking about. They are dangerously unrealistic." Larry Kirshbaum of Warner added, "In a sense, we are victims of our own expectations. We are victimized by our need to promote and hype a book to get it out into a bookselling system where there are already so many titles that one has to take a very aggressive stand in order to be noticed."

Another contributor to chronic author anxiety is increased communication among authors. Not only are the big deals being blared louder than ever before, but the means for disseminating the information are greater than ever, too. The growth of local and regional writers groups and the establishment of active organizations of professional writers have made it possible for authors to learn one another's business on a regular basis. Professional writers organizations have online bulletin boards enabling subscribers to network daily with one another. News of big deals and of the apotheosis of hot authors is instantly disseminated along with gossip and other chitchat and spreads like prairie fire on the tinder of insecurity that is so common a component of the emotional makeup of writers.

Organizations devoted to genre literature are particularly fertile breeding grounds for such insecurity because of the system of local, regional, and national conventions (and you can now find one every week of the year) that bring aspiring writers into contact with star authors. Conventions serve many vital functions for established and would-be authors, as well as for agents, editors, and fans. But they are also a perfect medium for the flourishing of invidious comparisons, especially because not all attendees are able to restrain the temptation to boast. Successful authors garner adulation at conventions, leaving the less recognized to brood over their neglect.

The envy phenomenon is by no means restricted to genre writers, however. "The literary cliques are hotbeds of jealousy," an agent commented to me. "It's subtle, though, because the literati like to think they're too civilized to indulge in such unbecoming emotions as jealousy. But if I pull off a good deal for one client, I can tell you I'm going to hear from half a dozen others by the end of the day. Naturally, they'll try to disguise their jealousy, the way the runner-up in a beauty contest does, but believe me, their message is loud and clear: How come you didn't do that for me?" The professional marriage of superagents Mort Janklow and Lynn Nesbit precipitated a tremendous outpouring of anxiety among authors, both clients and nonclients of theirs, as the press proclaimed that only authors represented by star agents had a chance of survival in today's marketplace. The cover story of the *New York Times Magazine* was dedicated to the Janklow-Nesbit marriage, occasioning a cartoon in *Publishers Weekly* suggesting that agents should now do book signings in stores instead of authors, since their deals are more newsworthy than the contents of the books they sell.

The jealousy of authors puts pressure on agents and publishers to exceed each other's achievements. Operating on the principle that the squeaky wheel gets oiled, author demands for bigger advances, print runs, advertising guarantees, and other advantages are often granted by publishers. But their motive for doing so is as often the fear of losing the author as it is a sincere desire to reward strong sales performances on previous books. In other words, the ability to bully becomes a prized virtue in an agent. But while bullying is certainly a valid tactic for agents to apply under circumstances, its employment as a policy can be detrimental to a client in the long run, and its adoption by all agents as a defensive strategy to prevent one another from capturing each other's authors, can be fatal to the writing and publishing professions.

It has to be faced that some books merit more commitment than others. Or that publishers feel more enthusiastic about some books on their lists than they do about others. Or that a publisher has reached its realistic price ceiling and cannot go a dime higher without damaging its profit structure. Or that it has spent all of its season's budget on advertising and must restrain its outlay for certain titles. If agents respond to these realities by picking up their marbles and taking them elsewhere, then their clients' interests may not always be best served. Unfortunately, the agent who counsels reason and patience in such cases is in jeopardy of losing clients to any agent who claims he can plunder publishers better than his colleagues can. "It's like the logging industry," one publisher observed. "You can make huge profits cutting down all the trees in the forest, but what are you doing to the environment? And where will the next generation of trees come from?"

In today's publishing climate it is all but impossible for authors to assess the value of their work without comparing it to what others get for (what they perceive to be) the same type of work and the same circumstances. In truth, the conditions affecting every negotiation are unique, no matter how similar they may appear on the surface. I could list a hundred factors, from the very obvious, like author track record, to the very subtle, such as the weather, without exhausting the possible ingredients that go into a deal. But insecure authors don't always appreciate such fine distinctions. Instead, they see only the realization of their worst nightmare: that *somebody is better than they are.* "That idea," says agent Russell Galen, "is intolerable to most authors, and we must constantly reassure them that it is not a matter of who's better and who's worse."

The agents I spoke with were unanimous in insisting that no two authors are identical when it comes to treatment by agents or publishers. "I emphasize that we are involved in a long-term process," says Galen. "You have to think in terms of a career and not on a book-to-book basis. If you don't get as much as the other guy today, you'll get more than the other guy tomorrow." Says another agent, "If you'll just keep your nose over your typewriter and stop worrying about what everyone else is doing, you'll eventually get your turn."

The frenzy surrounding headline-making deals, with its attendant author stampede mentality, must eventually throw our values completely out of kilter. In reaction to a *New York Times Magazine* article about literary agents, one hopeful author wrote, "Break-even points, bottom lines, last dollars, seven-figure sales—all of this sounds very much like the 'only big hits' frenzy that has resulted in the demise of Broadway theater. Fewer and fewer demographically marketed manuscripts are making more and more money for fewer and fewer people, and the creative artists be damned. After all, isn't the joy of merely *writing* all the reward a writer needs?" Apparently, the answer to that question is, increasingly, no, and that is cause for the utmost distress. For when authors are distracted from the work at hand by anxieties of inferiority; when their zest for writing is spoiled by worries about status; when they invest more energy into showing up their fellow authors than they do in creating things of truth and beauty; then surely our literature must suffer.

"Where is their pride?" an older agent lamented to me. "Where is their dignity?" His words touched the essence of the matter for me. The writing profession used to stand for pride and dignity, but these seem to be succumbing to the mad warfare of mergers and takeovers, and it's a valid cause for worry. If there are any values worth pitting against the juggernaut of the numbers game, they are the pride and dignity of the solitary author at his machine, wresting meaning from chaos, pleasure from pain, and elegance from sordid reality. They're old-fashioned virtues, but I'd like to see them preserved.

■

Found Money

IN 1965, A YOUNG HARVARD LAWYER named Ralph Nader launched his war for public safety when he brought out his book, *Unsafe at Any Speed.* Some seven years later, a young freelance writer named Richard Curtis published a juvenile biography of Nader. The former book went on to become a classic in the literature of reform. The latter drifted to the bottom of the sea of anonymity—until recently. It so happens that I was approached by a small publisher of children's books, and the editor made me an offer to reissue my Nader biography. The deal was modest, but I grabbed it: it was found money. Then I started reflecting on one of the most pleasant benefits inuring to authors, the recycling of their books, articles, and stories.

The selling of anthology, translation, movie, and other ancillary rights to their clients' literary properties is second nature to agents. So, it's easy for us to forget how gratifying it is for an author to see his or her story appear in a grade school reader, where it is actually *studied* by children as if it were Dickens or Twain. Or how charming it is to read the opening page of a translation of one's novel, to realize that people in Finland or Greece or Japan are reading it, too. Or how satisfying it is to know that a work published ten or twenty years ago has been deemed worthy of revival, of stimulating a new generation of readers, and perhaps of enduring beyond one's own lifetime.

The reissue of books published early in their careers is a matter of great interest to many authors. One of the commonest questions I hear is, Can you resell my old books? It's a short question that deserves a long answer, for there is more resistance to reissues, even reissues of books by big-name authors, than most writers imagine.

Although we all would love to see our books become backlist classics, earning royalties year in and year out for ourselves and our heirs, the realities of modern-day publishing militate against longevity for all but a handful of works of fiction and nonfiction each year. Today's emphasis on frontlist publishing—the bestseller mentality that stresses big and fast successes enabling publishers to recover their investments quickly—has reduced the lives of most popular books to something barely observable in an atomic bubble chamber. In paperback books, particularly, the turnover in merchandise is frighteningly rapid. The average paperback novel does not remain on a shelf as long as a box of Hostess Twinkies.

Alert authors and agents monitor the sales activity of their books, and as soon as they detect a fibrillating pulse, they request reversions of rights, recapturing their property in order to sell it to other publishers. Many of them discover, however, that the market for once-published books is surprisingly weak. Most publishers would prefer to buy an original book for $5,000 or $10,000 than a reissue for a fraction of these prices. Obviously, factors other than economic are at play here.

The most important is the fame or obscurity of the author. Writers who achieve success create curiosity and interest in everything else that they have ever brought out, and in that case, it does make sense to republish earlier works. Smaller or underfinanced publishers desirous of having a big name on their lists will occasionally buy some early effort by that author, dress it up in a nice package, put the author's name in large letters, and send it out into the light of day after decades of out-of-print neglect—a neglect often well deserved, by the way.

Another critical factor is the amount of time between editions of a book. Despite the fact that the earlier edition came out in a small printing that lived no longer than a swarm of May flies, publishers seem to feel that a decade or longer must pass before a new generation of readers will support a reissue. Also, many paperback houses (and the reissue business is almost totally a paperback one) will not consider publishing what they disdainfully refer to as a "retread" unless it is accompanied by a new and original work by the same author. That way, they can use the publicity about the new book as a crutch to support the old one.

Reissues, then, are by no means the automatic sales that many authors believe them to be. Nevertheless, it is sound business practice to recover the rights to your old books as soon as it is feasible to do so. If there is no market for them today, you simply hold them against a day when there will be. You may become famous, thus creating a demand for anything with your name on it. And because the prices paid for works by famous authors are higher than those paid for un- and little-knowns, the reverted books you "bank" today may well be appreciating in value dramatically, if quietly, like a painting bought at a garage sale that turns out to be an old master.

Sometimes it's not the author who becomes famous but the subject matter. Just as some common household objects of today become the valuable artifacts of tomorrow, some books become hot properties only after future events make them so. One of the first books I sold as an agent was about the psychic power of pyramids. After strutting and fretting its brief hour upon the stage, no more was heard of it until very recently. The revival of New Age subjects made that book a perfect candidate for reissue.

You should not expect publishers to be particularly cooperative with your efforts to salvage your old books. For one thing, they too are hoping that you will become famous. Then the rights to your early books will be in *their* accounts rather than yours. Good publishers try to keep books in print as long as possible because backlist publishing can be a low-cost, high-profit operation. Although many books barely eke out a profit on their first runs, the economics of subsequent printings shift heavily in the publisher's favor. Publishers, therefore, comb their backlists looking for suitable reissue prospects.

If there is no valid reason for bringing a book out again, a publisher will probably place it on the back burner until the author or agent asks for the rights back, and even then it may take some pestering and pressuring before the publisher relinquishes its grip. Applications for reversions of rights take low priority for most publishers because the process requires some research and analysis of sales figures and other factors that determine whether the embers can and should be blown back into flame.

One of the biggest hindrances to the recycling of books is outdatedness. Fiction can become outdated in themes, language, and attitudes that fix works to an earlier time. Issues that were hot may now seem quaint, styles of dress and coiffure that once were appropriate are now laughable, assumptions taken for granted have long since proven unworkable. In some cases, these faults can be corrected by revision, but in others, the book must stand as an anachronism, and any publisher interested in reissuing it must accept it—and ask the reader to accept it—for what it is, an exhibit in the museum of an author's creative development. Not all books profit from updating.

Nonfiction presents some interesting contrasts in durability. Some types, such as history or biography, may endure forever, particularly if the subject is one that posterity keeps alive. There are works whose lives may be extended by occasional updating, and still others that are miraculously brought back from the dead by cyclical trends in reader interest. A good example of a book that enjoyed two rich lives is *Profiles in Courage* by John F. Kennedy, which won a Pulitzer Prize before its author achieved political prominence, then was rejuvenated when Kennedy became president of the United States.

On the other hand, nonfiction addressed to a timely topic may never be appropriate for reissue: campaign biographies, for example, or fad diet books. In certain types of nonfiction, revised editions are a source of tremendous profit, and contractual language that an author may not have paid much attention to can profoundly affect his or her fortune. Technical, medical, legal, and scientific textbooks may require updating every couple of years or even annually, and more popular books may have to be spruced up from time to time to keep up with changing times. A book I represented years ago, *How to Start and Manage Your Own Small Business,* has been updated several times to reflect new types of businesses that did not exist when the book was originally published, changes in tax legislation, shifts in consumer attitudes, perceptions, and so on. The provisions of your contract that control the way these revisions are effectuated and compensated may be booby-trapped and must be scrutinized.

In the first place, the decision as to whether a revision is desirable is usually strictly at the publisher's sole discretion. Although the original author usually has the option to do the revisions him- or herself, the author who cannot or does not wish to revise his book may not have a great deal to say about it if his publisher takes a tough stand and demands that a revision be undertaken. If the author does agree to do the revisions himself, there is seldom language in the contract stipulating what he will be paid. Indeed, the language of most revision clauses I have examined would imply that the publisher expects the writer to do the revision for nothing.

If the author cannot or will not do the revision himself, his contract grants his publisher the right to assign the job to an outside writer, a person who may be unknown to the author and incompetent to perform the task. The compensation for this outside editorial work is determined solely at the publisher's discretion, and is deductible from the author's royalties. What is worse, in many cases the publisher is entitled by the terms of its contract to reduce the author's royalties in ever-growing increments for each revision that the author himself does not perform, and to give byline credit to the outside reviser. Thus, after several revisions, the author may lose much or even most of his stake in his own book, and some of the credit for it as well.

Finally, most revision clauses for nonfiction books state that for purposes of royalty computation, the revised edition shall be considered a new work. That means that if you have an escalating royalty scale, it will drop back to the base percentage every time your publisher brings out a revised edition. If, for example, your royalty scale starts at 10 percent on the first five thousand copies sold, then slides up to 12½ percent on the next five thousand, then 15 percent on all copies sold thereafter, the royalty on your revised edition will drop back to 10 percent. As production costs for new editions are by no means low, this provision is not unfair by any means. But it does contain the potential for depriving an author of some royalty income if the revisions are superficial and production costs on the new edition are not high.

It's a good idea, then, to negotiate some system of compensation for revisions at the time you are negotiating your original contract. Perhaps a pro rata percentage of your original advance should be payable to you for the ratio of revised material to original material. In any event, if you do accept that a revised or updated edition is necessary, always agree to do it yourself. If you can't actually perform the task, you can farm it out to someone of your own choosing and thus control both the quality of the material and the cost of revising it. If that is not feasible, then at least negotiate the right to approve the outside reviser selected by your publisher, and to have some control or consultation over that person's compensation. The reduction of your royalties and alteration of your byline should be effected only with your express approval. You should also be mindful of the following:

- Never sell your copyright outright if you can help it.
- Get reversions to every book of yours that goes out of print, however unlikely a candidate for reissue you may think it to be.
- Keep the reversion language in your contracts as tight as possible. Try to grant rights to your publisher for a specific number of years, with reversion to occur automatically at the end of that term. If your publisher's contract states that you may request a reversion of rights if your book goes out of print after x years, negotiate the lowest possible value for x. Three years is a good number to aim for.
- Negotiate as many free copies as possible when you make your

original deal, or buy as many copies as you may need for a lifetime. That way, you will always have copies to submit to publishers when you solicit interest in reissues.

And let us not forget the most important rule of all when it comes to getting your work reissued: *Become famous.*

■

The Two Worlds of Literature

$\mathbb{A}$BOUT ONCE A DECADE, SOME member of the intelligentsia launches an attack on one literary genre or another, setting off vitriolic debate about the legitimacy of popular fiction. Perhaps the most famous of these outbursts was critic Edmund Wilson's assault on mystery literature, "Who Cares Who Killed Roger Ackroyd?" In October 1985, the conflict fulminated again with a particularly nasty broadside aimed at science fiction and published in *Harper's* magazine. The writer termed the genre "detritus" and "the domain of hobbyists and hacks," and argued that "science fiction has become a dead zone useful for dumping space travel, extraterrestrials, weird inventions, time warps, extrasensory perception, biological mutations, the morals of intelligent machines, and anything else that would be of genuine scientific interest were it not fictional."

This sally provoked a firestorm of retaliatory letters from practitioners of the genre, and, as far as I am concerned, these consigned the essay to the garbage heap it so aptly deserved. My own revenge is to invoke journalistic privilege by declining to utter here the name of the perpetrator. But the episode did stimulate some thoughts about the age-old war between the intellectual establishment and the world of popular literature, and I would like to express them.

When I went into the publishing business after graduating from college, I discovered a literary culture so vastly different from the ones I had studied that I could scarcely find any common ground between them. This world was populated by romance, science fiction and fantasy, and male action-adventure writers; by pulpsters, pornographers, and countless others who earn their livings producing genre books.

Since then I have become a citizen of that world, both as a writer and as a literary agent representing other writers of category fiction. I have come to know and respect, to admire and even love this world and its denizens. I have had the privilege of attending the birth of some works that have come to be regarded as masterpieces of their genres. During this period of twenty-five years, I have become increasingly concerned about how little is known about this world by the writers and critics who dominate the world of serious literature. And I've concluded that we are all a little poorer for these gaps in awareness, appreciation, and communication.

The belletristic establishment regards the world of popular literature as a subculture, but one could seriously argue that it is really the other way around. Very few "serious" writers make enough money from their writing to support themselves without having to moonlight. Their audiences are often modest in size and elitist in taste. Their work is frequently inaccessible, intellectual, experimental, and sometimes incomprehensible. Literary authors are often isolated from their fellow writers both physically and artistically, so that they have little sense of community or opportunities for intellectual cross-pollination.

Now look at the world of genre literature. Its purveyors are professional authors, most of whom earn a comfortable living and many of whom earn a substantial one—all without having to rely on nonwriting jobs to supplement their incomes. These authors reach a wide audience. Because many write original paperbacks, they can count on a minimum readership numbering in the hundreds of thousands and even millions. Their prose style and craftsmanship range from competent (they must at least be competent to sell their work to publishers) to superb; I will stake my career on the assertion that the craftsmanship and prose to be found in the best genre books matches or exceeds that found in the work of many so-called literary stars.

Professional writers enjoy a strong sense of cohesiveness and mutual support that is lacking in the world of belles lettres. Professional science-fiction, western, romance, and mystery writers belong to guildlike organizations that publish newsletters, hold conventions, and lobby for improvement of terms and conditions for their constituent authors. Taken altogether, these factors suggest that the life of the professional writer is far better integrated into the social fabric than that of the literary author. Genre writers might be likened to the guild artisans of medieval times, with the exception that the medieval craftsmen had the respect of their peers and patrons and were completely integrated into the community.

I have frequently pondered what it is that separates these two worlds of literary endeavor, and can think of a number of elements. One is *ideas.* The world of serious literature stresses the primacy of ideas, and the format of serious literature is designed to express those ideas. Another critical element is *viewpoint.* the serious author's viewpoint, or vision, is what makes those ideas fresh and special. And then there is *style,* the unique garb in which the author's ideas are dressed. We are able to identify the most interesting authors after a page or two because of what they have to say and how they say it. All too often, however, that format is not accessible to the mass reader because it doesn't follow the universal verities that, as Aristotle contended, humankind supposedly responds to. It is sometimes remote, dislocated, overly stylized, tedious, or just plain badly constructed and expressed. But the author, and presumably his or her audience, doesn't necessarily care, as long as the essential idea is conveyed in a stimulating way.

Few professional authors approach their work this way; not, at least, if they want to stay in business. In the value system of the professional author, the most important element is story, for stories are what pros are paid to write, and the ones who are paid the most are those who write the best stories and write stories best. Ideas may be articulated, certainly, but only insofar as they help delineate the viewpoint of the characters themselves. Professional authors seldom allow their own ideas or viewpoint to override those of the characters who people their books, and the idea of calling attention to themselves through unique stylistic techniques is totally alien to them. Indeed, if a professional novelist slows the pace of his book to express some personal viewpoint, or distracts the reader's involvement with his story by employing stylistic gimmicks, he can expect his editor to come down very hard on the offending passage with a blue pencil. Totally unlike serious literature, it is often impossible, upon reading a popular novel, to guess who the author is, so well disguised is he or she behind the excellence of the tale itself. And that is the way that they, their publishers, and their readers like it.

The lives of professional genre writers differ in many significant ways from those of their more literary brothers and sisters, and indeed from the romantic image so many people have of the way writers are supposed to live. They are, for example, extremely businesslike, or at least extremely concerned with the business of writing. They study the provisions of their publishing contracts carefully, and actively consult with their agents in the negotiating dialogues with publishers. They know the market value of their work before they sell it, sometimes within $500 or $1,000, and, in fact, most of them sell their work before they write it, lining up contracts (often for more than one book at a time) in advance. They approach the work at hand in a businesslike fashion as well. Because genre book lines have specific word-length requirements to fit them into the publishers' rigid price and marketing structures, genre writers have to design their manuscripts to those lengths and to pace the development and dramatic flow of their books so that all is resolved within 60,000, 75,000, or 100,000 words.

Which leads us to another quality of the professional writer: discipline. Inspiration, as it is commonly understood, plays little part in the life of the genre author, for, as we have seen, ideas are subordinate to the story in the author's value system. Having selected a milieu or location, outlined a story, and sketched the cast of characters, the writer then tackles the job the way a skilled carpenter might approach the building of a piece of furniture, day by day, piece by piece. Of paramount importance is the outline. The synopses of genre books are often highly detailed and broken down chapter by chapter or even scene by scene, so that every day, when a writer sits down at her desk, she knows precisely what work is cut out for her. It is here, in the daily task of writing the book itself, that inspiration plays a role. As the author follows her outline, the nuances of character, the details of time and place, the fine points of story and complications of plot flow endlessly onto the page from a source that is wondrous and mystifying. Characters take on lives and wills of their own, struggling with the author for control of the work (and sometimes, to her astonishment, winning). This day-to-day grind with its little pleasures, epiphanies, and triumphs may not be as romantic as the big bang variety of inspiration we usually associate with art, but it does enable professional writers to get their work done no matter how ill, rotten, depressed, exhausted, or bereft of spirit they may feel on any given day. "You turn it on," they will tell you, "and out it comes." Writer's block is therefore seldom a problem for professional authors, and besides, it's a luxury they cannot afford.

These writers know pretty much to the word how much they can write daily before growing fatigued: two thousand words, say, or twenty manuscript pages, or three chapters, whatever it may be, of work that is consistently good, often good enough to be acceptable in a single draft. They can therefore predict almost to the day when they will be turning in their manuscripts to their publishers. This is critically important both from an author's own viewpoint—in order to project income flow—and from the publisher's, for the firm must be able to count on reliable production in order to schedule books far in advance with relative confidence. Because covers and monthly catalogues are produced by paperback publishers before manuscripts are actually in hand and salespeople solicit orders months before publication, the failure of an author to deliver a book on schedule is a nightmare that haunts paperback editors. Reliability therefore becomes the prime virtue of professional writers.

Unlike so many literary authors, professional writers are intensely attuned to the demands of the literary marketplace, because their lives and livings depend on its fluctuations. Genres go in and out of style and heaven help the author who doesn't adapt to a trend. As I write, science fiction is doing okay, westerns are holding steady, the horror market is soft, mysteries are strong, and the demand for formula romances is good. Authors working in these fields are expected to know about these cycles, indeed, to know about nuances within the cycles: that within the science-fiction genre, fantasy is doing well except for the subspecies known as sword-and-sorcery; that in the romance genre, historicals are hard to place, romantic mystery is in demand, and sexy contemporaries are still salable.

Like professionals in other fields of endeavor, professional writers exchange information with each other about the state of their fields. They belong to organizations devoted specifically to their genres, such as the Science Fiction Writers of America, Mystery Writers of America, Western Writers of America, and Romance Writers of America. These organizations regularly publish newsletters profiling leading writers in their fields, offering market reports about which publishers are buying what material, how much they're paying, and whom to contact. Annual national conventions (and frequent regional ones as well) are held where organization members exchange information, conduct seminars, meet agents and editors, and honor their own for achievements in various categories. These meetings are usually well attended by representatives of the publishing industry and offer writers and editors an opportunity to conduct business on a less formal basis than is customary.

While I realize I've painted a black-and-white picture, discussions I've had with countless numbers of writers in all fields strongly suggest that the polarity of admiration and emulation runs from genre writers to mainstream ones, but not vice versa. Oh, from time to time a mainstream author will confess a secret passion for genre fiction that can be likened to a craving for junk food; and on occasion a mainstream author will cross over into genre fiction by writing a science-fiction or mystery novel, a sort of literary equivalent of slumming. But these are exceptions that play up the rule that most literary authors don't feel genre writers have anything to say to them. That this is arrant snobbery goes without saying. I also happen to feel it is bad thinking.

The time has come for serious writers to pay far more attention to their genre colleagues than they have done up to now. The increasingly monolithic publishing industry now concentrates such power that the livelihoods and freedom of expression of writers of every kind are seriously threatened. As publishers focus more intently each year on producing blockbuster bestsellers to carry their bottom lines, the time and space in which writers can develop shrinks, meaning they are being forced to mature far too early. As the spawning grounds for writers get squeezed harder and harder by economic exigencies, the pressure on tenderly budding talents to turn out commercial successes becomes more and more intense. This disease has spread from giant bookstore chains to publishing conglomerates and has now infected the thinking of authors of every stripe, who feel their only choices are to hit the pot of gold on the first shot, or become computer programmers or insurance salespeople. When I entered the publishing business in 1959, a writer could still cherish—and achieve—the fantasy of a quiet life of literary accomplishment, a life in which one could be content with a modest living and the admiration of a small but dedicated audience. Today, this notion is so laughably out-of-date that I cannot imagine anyone seriously harboring it. More to the point is that if anybody did, it would be impossible to achieve it. And I believe there is worse ahead: As the conglomeratization of the publishing industry continues, it is possible that literature will no longer be a place in which writers achieve any dreams at all—save that of getting rich from writing stuff they don't give a damn about. If this vision seems excessively dark, you have only to listen to the complaints of television writers in order to foresee the future.

It is vital for the writing establishment to realize that literature is far more than a ladder with junk at the bottom and art at the top. Rather, it is an ecosystem in which the esoteric and the popular commingle, fertilize one another, and interdepend. Principally, if it were not for the immense revenues generated by science fiction, romance, male action-adventure, and other types of popular fiction which so many literary authors and critics look down their noses upon, there would be no money for publishers to risk on first novels, experimental fiction, and other types of serious but commercially marginal literary enterprises. Furthermore, from the aspect of the writing craft itself, there are many extremely important lessons for literati to learn from their genre comrades in arms, if only the former would take the trouble to study them. Although serious writers tend to reject formula plotting, for instance, they sooner or later realize that if they wish to reach any kind of audience at all, they will have to construct at least a minimum of formula skeleton for their works. When they do realize it, they have but to visit the popular-literature departments of their local bookstores to discover a trove of skillfully fashioned works to teach them about creating sympathetic heroes and heroines, daunting conflicts and antagonists, masterful pacing, and the building of dramatic tension to a thrilling climax and a satisfying ending.

And there is more: pride and professionalism, skill and discipline, reliability, attention to the business aspects of the writer's trade, a healthy respect for publishers and for the vast audiences that publishers speak for—these are among the lessons waiting to be learned by those on the other side of the gulf that separates the two worlds. Above all, writers stand to discover that they by no means have a monopoly on integrity. And because the integrity of all writers is now in jeopardy, it is incumbent on those of both worlds to talk and listen to each other, to read each other, and, above all, to respect each other.

■

Is There a Future?

Toward Reform

THE PUBLISHING INDUSTRY IS CRITI-
cally ailing, and no one, from the creator of the written word to the
consumer, is untouched. The signs are everywhere, some statistically
demonstrable, others less tangible but still manifest to anyone who
has been in the business long enough to watch it evolve. Some of the
more commonly voiced ones are the following:

- The conglomeratization of trade and paperback book publishing
- The bureaucratization of editorial decision making
- The "blockbuster mentality" and the increased dependence of
  publishers on big-name authors
- The insecurity and instability caused by the buying and selling
  of publishing companies
- The growth of bookstore chains, with their emphasis on current
  bestsellers
- The narrowing of publishers' profit margins
- The high prices of both hardcover and paperback books
- The diminution of new and experimental literature
- The soaring rate of books returned unsold to publishers

- The contrast between the modest advances and royalties paid to midlist authors and the staggering ones paid to superstars
- The increasing delays on settlement of advances and royalties with authors
- The decline of professional standards of line editing
- The failure of publishing to keep dedicated editors
- The influx of business administrators into publishing, and their influence on editorial policies
- The assertion by authors and agents that publishers are cheating them out of royalties

Obviously, there is no single comprehensive explanation of what has gone wrong, nor any all-embracing solution. Still, it is surprising that authors, agents, publishers, booksellers, and other book people, all highly intelligent individuals, should continue applying patches and poultices to the symptoms when it is clear that the dimensions of the problem call for a thorough reevaluation of the way things are done in the publishing industry.

Although I would not be so vain as to suggest I have a panacea, I would like to focus on what I feel is the essence of the matter: the way books are merchandised. And I will be so bold as to propose a plan for restoring health to the industry. It is a radical plan that calls for a new way of looking at how we do business and for cooperation among all the elements of the book community, from authors to booksellers. Whether my observations are on the mark or not, the issues they touch on are of tremendous importance and urgency to everyone in the publishing community, and like it or not, we will have to address them if that community and its magnificent tradition are to be preserved.

Book publishing may be big business in some ways, but its system of distribution is a ridiculously antiquated one. Unlike most other forms of manufacturing, the products, books, are sold on consignment. That is to say, the books are in effect loaned to wholesalers and retailers, and though they do pay publishers for their merchandise, they can get their money back (or at least credit) if consumers don't buy the books.

At best, this system is grossly inefficient, wasteful, costly, and risky. In its worst manifestations, however, it is pernicious and very close to fraudulent. Unsold books, under a consignment system, are a form of currency, and like any other form of currency, are subject to manipulation. It is well to keep this point in mind as we examine how business is conducted in publishing.

In times gone by, when money was looser and the book business was booming, consignment merchandising of books worked well enough in its dinosaur fashion. The publishing community shrugged resignedly and concluded that that's the way things have always been done and it would be too much trouble to change them. In the last few years, however, both the economy and the publishing industry have experienced severe downturns from which no robust or permanent recovery is on the immediate horizon. Battered by high costs that have driven book prices to the limits of consumer toleration, assailed by such tough competitors for discretionary dollars as movies and television, video games and interactive online activities, both publishers and bookstores have seen volume sales and profit margins erode year after year. In their increased eagerness to maintain cash flow, they have taken greater and greater advantage of the opportunities inherent in the old consignment system to bolster their financial positions.

The source of cash flow for the publishing industry is, of course, the book consumer. But whereas a few years ago the consumer thought little of spending $10.00 for a hardcover book or scooping up two or three $1.75 paperbacks at the airport newsstand, today, prices drifting toward $30.00 for routine hardcovers and $7.00 for routine mass-market paperbacks have caused the consumer to become cautious, selective, and resistant. He or she only spends money on blockbuster bestsellers, familiar big-name authors, formulaic imitations, or highly promoted titles. With cash receipts diminishing, bookstores frantically seek ways to generate capital and hold what capital they generate. Many prolong settlements with distributors and publishers and use the currency of returns to buy new merchandise. Publishers, in turn, stretch out settlements with authors or with other publishers (as in the case of paperback reprinters who owe money to hardcover publishers), and they often yield to the temptation to manipulate returns to generate funds. At every step of the way—from book buyer to book creator—cash is held as long as possible to earn interest or simply to settle the most urgent obligations.

There is nothing new about businesses holding money as long as they can in hard times. What does seem to be of recent vintage, however, is the use of the old consignment system as the principal source of cash. To put it simply, the returnability and refundability of books has become the chief means for publishers and booksellers to raise, keep, and earn interest on their money. This is possible because returns have risen steadily over the last few years and are now at an all-time high. Let's look at some tricks of the consignment trade and see exactly how it has become corrupted.

As we've seen, publishers are the prime beneficiaries of a system that requires unsold books to be returned for full credit. Because they presumably cannot predict what percentage of their books will be sold and what percentage returned, they establish a reserve fund when they collect money from booksellers; this fund is supposedly used to pay the booksellers for returned copies. Although the reserve is supposed to be, by virtue of the publisher's contract with the author, "reasonable," and the publisher usually has a good idea of what percentage of returns can be expected on any particular book or genre of books, publishers all too frequently hold far in excess of that reasonable figure.

Not only do they hold too much money, they hold it longer than they ought to, for although a book's sales picture usually emerges sharply after one year (indeed, the actual shelf life of most trade books and paperbacks can be measured in weeks), many publishers hold their reserves for years, releasing royalties at an unjustifiably slow rate. They often are able to accomplish such manipulations undetected because, until recently, few publishers' royalty statements stipulated the number of copies printed, distributed, or held as a reserve against returns, making it impossible for the recipient of these statements to understand, let alone argue with, them. ("If royalty statements were manuscripts," one editor confided to me, "I'd reject them.")

Unfortunately, many authors and agents don't understand publishing accounting practices and therefore don't even know what questions to ask; those who do are often fearful of reprisal. Hardcover publishers tend to be lax in demanding accountings from paperback publishers out of fear that the tables will be turned on them, for many hardcover publishers now are tied corporately to paperback publishers. Many hardcover publishers aggravate the hostility of authors and agents by never including in their own royalty statements copies of statements they receive from paperback reprinters, book clubs, or other sources of subsidiary revenue such as foreign publishers.

Although it is hard to sympathize with publishers, they happen to be the victims of creative bookkeeping as much as they are the perpetrators. Bookstores suffering cash-flow problems, for instance, have been known to manipulate the ordering, holding, and returning of books in such a way as to maximize their own cash position. Finding itself short of cash to buy a forthcoming blockbuster, for example, a bookstore might ship back to publishers unopened boxes of books the store considers marginal; or it might decide that now is the time to return some backlist books that haven't moved fast enough. Returns being a form of currency, the publishers must take these books back and give the stores the credit they need to buy that hot new bestseller. These practices only intensify the scramble for bestsellers and the concomitant drop of interest in new, experimental, and other less-than-commercial literature—what publishers derogatorily call midlist books—that have characterized book merchandising in the last twenty years.

Then there is the problem of overordering. Stores and chains frequently order unrealistically large numbers of copies of books they believe to be big hits—a practice encouraged, of course, by the publishers' salespeople. If a book is a big hit, the store has the stock to fill the demand. If not, the store can return the books for credit. Although publishers try to make it as hard as possible for stores to do so, it's still very little skin off the bookseller's nose to overorder in this no-lose situation. But for a publisher to print a large number of copies on the strength of heavy orders, then to suffer huge losses when the stores return their overstock in massive quantities, is both outrageously unprofitable and tragically wasteful.

Needless to say, the tensions, resentments, and suspicions created by these practices and subterfuges are terribly destructive to harmony among authors, publishers, and booksellers at a time when the spirit of cooperation has never been more desperately needed. Isn't it clear that the source of these antagonisms, the acid rain that is poisoning the delicate ecology of the publishing environment, is the system by which books may be returned for credit? Isn't it clear even from this general survey of the problems that the entire system is hopelessly antiquated and urgently in need of reform?

Over the last few years, publishers have talked about merchandising books on a nonreturnable basis, and a few have done something about it. Some of the bolder experiments, such as one attempted by Harcourt Brace Jovanovich, failed, though the endeavor was by no means a debacle. Generally speaking, these efforts failed for lack of cooperation among all the sectors of the publishing community. Specifically, they failed, first, because bookstores do not particularly like getting stuck with unsalable merchandise, and, second, because the discounts offered by publishers to induce booksellers to buy on a nonreturnable basis weren't high enough. If, however, publishers could raise their discounts substantially, perhaps the stores would feel less resistant to accepting merchandise now considered marginal, such as first novels, midlist books, experimental fiction, and slower-moving backlist books—literature that is now being frozen out of the marketplace by the blockbuster mentality.

But how can publishers possibly raise their discounts any higher than they already are without cutting even further into slim profit margins? With printing, paper, editorial and production, postage, and other costs sky-high, there doesn't seem to be anything left to trim. Or has something been overlooked?

As a matter of fact, something has. It happens to be authors' royalties. I believe they should be cut. Perhaps by as much as 50 percent.

Now, as that's the kind of statement that can get an agent strung up by his heels in the public square by a rabble of maddened authors, let me hasten to state the rest of the proposition: *Publishers should stop paying royalties on the number of copies sold and start paying them on the number of copies printed.* In other words, an author who now earns a 10 or 12 percent royalty on her books would earn 5 or 6 percent under the new arrangement, but instead of waiting for years (maybe forever) for her publishers to release the reserved royalties to her, she would collect royalties on the date of printing. On the date of publication, the publisher would simply furnish a copy of the printer's affidavit stating the number of copies printed, and pay the author 5 or 6 percent of the list price based on that number less whatever sum the publisher advanced to him at the time the contract was signed. If the book did well and the publisher went back to press for a new printing, the publisher would simply send the author another check when the copies came off the press. Publishers would then pass the savings along to booksellers in the form of deeper discounts—on the condition that the books they buy are not re-turnable.

Although this plan must sound totally alien to authors and publishers alike, there are precedents for it—both past and present. A number of foreign publishers structure deals this way today, and the arrangement has proven satisfactory to all parties. More significant, perhaps, is that a number of years ago, a major paperback publisher, Fawcett, offered this kind of deal, and I don't know of a single author who didn't grab it. When negotiating with authors or agents for books in its line of original paperbacks, Fawcett frequently proposed two alternatives to them. The first was a royalty of, say, 6 percent on the first 150,000 copies sold and 8 percent thereafter, to be calculated on the traditional basis of copies *sold;* the other, a lower royalty of 4 and 6 percent, was calculated on the number of copies *printed.* The authors who chose the latter were usually satisfied with it on all counts. Payments were prompt and dependable, the bookkeeping was elementary, and because proof of the number of copies printed was furnished with royalty checks, any suspicion that the publishers were cheating was completely allayed.

Everyone made out well under the Fawcett scheme. The key was the authors. The publishers understood something very important about them: most authors would rather get $1,000 now, without hassle, than gamble on the hope of collecting $1,500 over four or five years. When you analyze it, there is no difference between getting 8 percent royalty on 50,000 copies printed less 50 percent returned, and a 4 percent royalty on *all* 50,000 copies printed.

Eventually, Fawcett discontinued this arrangement. One reason, I suspect, is that authors and agents got greedy and decided that since 6 and 8 percent is more than 4 and 6 percent, they would eschew the printing-based royalty in favor of the sales-based royalty. At that time, when return rates were much lower than they are today, that must have made sense. But as return rates soared to the 50 and 60 percent levels at which they are today, authors and agents realized they were no better off than they had been under the old setup, and, in fact, they were worse off because rising return rates enabled publishers to justify holding enormous reserve royalties as a hedge against returns. One reason Fawcett may have been all too agreeable to do away with printing-based royalty accounting is that they, like all other publishers, recognized how much money was to be made on the "float," as bankers call it—the time it takes for money belonging to depositors to clear the system. In this case, the author is the depositor (it's his or her money, after all), and the time it takes for the author's money to clear the system is years—the time it's held until all returns are in and reserved royalties released. During that time, publishers can invest that money in interest-bearing securities, and the interest they bear does not go to the author, you can be sure.

Perhaps more importantly, Fawcett's arrangement was discontinued because of pressure by stores to return unsold books. The Fawcett plan was radical enough, *but it had not been adopted by the entire publishing industry.* Publishers would save immense amounts of money on printing, warehousing, freight, and bookkeeping costs (remember, to calculate royalties based on printings, you need one bookkeeper, one pad, one pencil, and one adding machine). Bookstores would effect similar savings and could invest them in the creation of remainder outlets.

I am proposing a return to the system of royalties based on printings, and although publishing people I have discussed this matter with have raised some objections, it is clear to me that the advantages far outweigh the potential disadvantages. Indeed, this may be the only solution in which nobody will be the loser and everyone—author, agent, publisher, bookseller, and even the consumer—wins.

From the author's viewpoint:

- Authors would receive royalties earlier than they do now
- Authors would receive no less royalties than they do now
- Knowing when and approximately how much royalties were due, authors would be able to budget their income more reliably
- Authors would become less suspicious of publishers' royalty accounting practices

From the publisher's viewpoint:

- Print runs would be more realistic
- Marketing of books would become more efficient
- Royalty accounting would be simplified substantially, creating savings in bookkeeping personnel and supporting overhead
- Money saved on lower royalty rates would be applied toward raising discounts to booksellers high enough to make a non-return arrangement less resistible
- Antagonism between publishers and authors-agents would be reduced greatly

From the bookseller's viewpoint:

- Because of higher discounts, the cost of stock would be reduced
- Wasteful overordering or overshipping would be reduced
- All expenses connected with returning books would be eliminated
- Unsold hardcover books would be more easily remaindered; instead of being returned to publishers and, in turn, sold back to remainder jobbers, these books would remain in the stores and be placed on sale
- Hostility between booksellers and publishers would be reduced

And from the consumer's viewpoint:
- More books would be available at discounted prices, and more at remainder prices as well
- Good backlist books would remain in stores, available to readers, for longer periods, helping to reverse the blockbuster mentality that now tends to sweep everything out of stores except current bestsellers
- Availability of heavily marked-down books (books that are now returned or stripped of their covers and pulped) would give lower-income consumers access to them, helping to raise literacy levels

When I first conceived this plan, I issued a challenge to all publishers to try this experiment. Almost every one of them felt threatened by it, because the way things are structured today, the only way to sell a thousand copies of a book is to print two thousand. The new scheme would compel them to print more conservatively. Given the destruction of our forests to feed the crazy system of overprinting that governs the publishing industry today, would not such restraint be welcome?

I did get one taker for what was dubbed the Curtis Plan. Tor Books made a deal with me for *Artifact,* a novel by Gregory Benford. Unfortunately, the results were inconclusive because the success of my scheme requires it to be adopted by a publisher across the board, and not just for one book. Indeed, it really requires adoption by the industry, a new way of thinking, marketing, distributing.

What publishers are really worried about is that if they cut their printings and stop flooding stores with books, their competitors will steal their rack space. This is precisely the kind of thinking that has gotten us into the current mess. *The entire industry* must shift to a nonreturnable standard, so that no publisher will be able to gain that kind of competitive edge. Could it be any worse than paying extortionate incentives to bookstore chains?

I'm certainly not going to hold my breath waiting for it to happen. But my challenge is still on the table.

The replacement of the consignment system of selling books is the publishing industry's most pressing need. We must, however, take a longer view, for in the long run, a structure based on delivering bound books to stores in motor vehicles is doomed. Amidst this crumbling infrastructure, a new one based on the electronic delivery of information is springing to life. I say "long run," yet the technology for producing handheld electronic reading devices is all but upon us. What is not yet upon us is a mind-set that will liberate our society from its dependency on words printed upon paper.

On the first wave of enthusiasm about the new media early in the 1990s, a number of publishers developed one variant or another on the so-called living book, a computerized reading device capable of "playing" digitized books and other texts such as newspapers and magazines. Unfortunately, such vital components as high compression, bright screen resolution, and portability were not sufficiently advanced, and several pioneers in the field fell on hard times. Most publishers gave up on the idea, and computer manufacturers, believing that no one was interested in a simple, single-function device like a book reader, went spinning off with digitized appointment calendars that send faxes while measuring your jogging heart rate and downloading your e-mail all at the same time.

It is time to revisit the living book, for it spells the salvation of the publishing industry. Picture a device the size of a book plugged into your wall socket for recharging of its battery, and into your phone jacket for downloading of any work available in digitized form, from today's newspaper to a novel published thirty years ago that is out of print in paper form. Picture reading these from a screen as bright as the page of today's conventional books, carrying it on the bus or subway, beach, bed, or bathtub. The problem of limited choice will have been eliminated, for publishers have their entire backlist in the memory storage of their central computer; each use debits the consumer's charge-card number and credits publisher and author with a royalty.

Picture a classroom of students inserting read-only memory cards in their readers containing selections from the curriculum. If they don't understand a word, a stroke of the key brings up a dictionary definition, and with another stroke, the book pronounces the troubling word aloud.

The development of the electronic reading device, and its adoption by the publishing industry and consumer, is, in my opinion, the top priority in any program for turning the book business around.

■

The Client from Hell: A Short Story

BECAUSE I HOLD MYSELF RESPON-
sible in large measure for the imminent destruction of our planet, I'm
writing this hasty narrative of my role in order for survivors, if any,
to read. To increase the odds that it will be discovered, I will send it
out over every electronic network I can log onto, requesting all users
to download it and place the hard copy in a fireproof container, as I
will be doing.

I'm not sure what benefit to future generations I expect this
account to produce. If, after thousands of years of recorded history,
humanity hasn't grasped the lesson that every war is the product of
folly, I can't imagine what it will take to convince us. Obviously, the
reduction of our globe to a cinder isn't dramatic enough to prove the
point.

"Folly" is too mild a word for the chain of events that brought us
to this pass, so I leave it to my reader to come up with one that aptly
describes how the human race turned its first encounter with extraterrestrial aliens from a historic opportunity to a debacle that has no
precedents, I am certain, in the history of the universe.

The visit of Garto and the Drunians to our world has been so thoroughly documented in every medium that I will not tire the reader with needless repetition. Instead I will include with this letter a copy of Garto's autobiography and a videotape of the television movie adaptation. As I place them in the box, I permit myself an ironic smile, for it is these very items that have led us to the brink of incineration.

On the day it was reported that a spaceship had touched down in New Guinea, I was scheduled to have lunch with one of my oldest friends in the publishing business, Bob Gorenstein of Random House. The news had come over the radio and because of the remoteness of the location, the only eyewitness account had been phoned in by the Masefields, the family whose plantation had been flattened by the six hundred ton mass of the Drunians' "travel disk." I doubt if anyone on our planet within earshot of a radio or television talked about anything else that morning, and, in fact, by noon the first of an endless crop of alien jokes was already bouncing over the phone lines between Hollywood and New York. And so, when Bob called me that morning to set up our lunch, he was ready with his quip.

"I'm surprised to find you in," he said. "I thought you'd already be on a plane to New Guinea to sign these guys."

"I hate representing celebrities," I said. "Even celebrities from outer space."

"What do you have against celebrities?"

"They're impossibly demanding."

"That's certainly true," said Gorenstein. "But I can't believe you'd turn down an opportunity to be the literary agent for the first alien visitors in the history of the world."

"I'm sure they're as big a pain in the ass as any other stars, plus they probably smell bad."

Bob booked lunch at one o'clock at An American Place on East 32nd Street, where we continued our banter over drinks. Shortage of time prohibits me from detailing these exchanges, which are irrelevant anyway. Suffice it to say that publishing people are among the wittiest of any profession, and there was much hilarity as we invented scenarios for such things as alien author tours, publishing parties, and talk-show interviews.

As Gorenstein donned his reading glasses to review the menu, he flashed a provocative smile. "Buddy Alter is already on his way to Papua."

I shook my head. "Why am I not surprised to hear this?" Buddy Alter stood at the purple end of the spectrum of literary agents, a true parasite who battened on the very worst that human nature had to offer. The moment a news story broke about some lurid murder, sex scandal, or tragedy, Buddy booked a plane to persuade the principals to let him handle their book, movie, and allied merchandise rights. And he didn't particularly care whether he represented perpetrator or victim. Buddy was the literary agent equivalent of an ambulance chaser.

A twinkle in Gorenstein's eyes told me there was something more. An instant later I guessed what it was. "And I suppose Random House has agreed to buy the book from Buddy if he comes back with their exclusive story."

Gorenstein smiled, not very cryptically. "The salmon special sounds very good."

"God almighty, Bob," I said, pounding the table. The china and silver jangled and the hubbub around us died for a moment as heads turned to the source of the disruption.

"Have you no shame?" I murmured after the noise level rose again.

Gorenstein chuckled. "We've only bought a right of first refusal," he said, summoning our waiter.

Thus began what might be called the Great Alien Sweepstakes, for, as it turned out, Buddy Alter was but one of a veritable tsunami of media representatives that swept across the Pacific Ocean that week hoping not merely to witness humanity's first confirmed encounter with members of a nonhuman race, but to tie up the exclusive rights to their story. The New Guinea government attempted to cordon off the site until it was established that the "alien blokes" were neither hostile nor contagious. But even the best armed military contingent is no match for a determined and resourceful television crew or an aggressive team of newspaper reporters. Certainly, the army was no match for the likes of Buddy Alter and his vision of fabulous commissions. It is said he had actually brought his checkbook with him! In what currency? I wondered.

I watched this circus on television and could only shake my head, as I had all during that lunch with Bob Gorenstein while I listened to him justifying his company's decision to get involved in the bidding war.

I suppose my reluctance to jump into this feeding frenzy will puzzle the reader, just as it did my colleagues in the publishing industry. It's a sign of the times that nobody even tried to understand how appalling I found it that people would cast their dignity to the winds to cash in on this event. Realizing that anything I said would sound like sour grapes, I said very little at all, but not a few colleagues thought that my attitude was insufferably smug.

Even my wife suggested I was foolish not to make at least some effort to offer the visitors representation."Wouldn't they be better off in your hands than in Buddy Alter's? My God, he'll have them endorsing Miller Lite Beer!"

We had just clicked off the evening news with the latest report on the carnival in New Guinea. Two executives from the Disney Company had offered to transport the spaceship to a site in Texas and create a 10,000-acre theme park around it.

"Not you, too," I moaned.

My wife gazed crossly at me. "Sometimes you wave your dignity around like some crusader's sword. Would it be so terrible for you to make an effort to contact them? Or have you suddenly become allergic to big commissions?"

This last remark stung me."I thought you understood how I feel."

"Why don't you run it past me once again to make sure."

"The whole thing is . . . well, so undignified," I said.

She peered at me. "The agent for the Butcher of Harlem is suddenly donning the mantle of dignity?"

"I didn't solicit him," I replied feebly.

She scowled. "I see. It's dignified to represent a man who slaughtered and cannibalized fifteen geriatric females because *he* solicited you. But it's *infra dignitatem* to solicit a voyager from another star."

"I feel like a prostitute when I chase authors."

"Your nobility is inspiring," she snorted, snapping a newspaper open and terminating the conversation.

I lapsed into a funk. Gazing at the ceiling with its spiderweb tracery of hairline cracks, I brooded on the unfairness of a world that handsomely rewarded prostitutes like Buddy Alter with penthouse apartments, second homes in the Hamptons, and Rolls Royces, but rewarded virtuous fellows like me with cramped apartments, seven-year-old Fords, and wives who had not enjoyed a genuine vacation in eight years.

Ultimately, I stood stoutly on my moral superiority and opted for the role of spectator. My wife, God bless her, never said another word about the matter. She didn't have to. Her feelings were painfully implicit in her sighs and baleful looks every time the news carried another story of the bidding wars for the Drunians' exclusive story, product endorsements, or participation in one commercial scheme or another.

After two or three months, however, it began to be apparent that no one had succeeded in signing the spacefarers. Newspaper accounts and media industry gossip indicated that the Drunians were being extremely wary. Whether out of confusion or distrust, it was not yet clear. Whatever motivated them, they definitely were not biting at offers that would have made even Michael Jordan envious. Their caution should not have come as such a surprise. Anyone sophisticated enough to develop a means of interstellar propulsion must presumably be shrewd enough to know when he is being hustled. As my Random House friend observed, "Hell, their race is twenty million years old, so we know they weren't born yesterday." He was one of innumerable shell-shocked veterans of the bidding wars returning to corporate headquarters with nothing to show for months in the field but a lot of bills for airfare, hotel accommodations, bar tabs, and diarrhea medicine.

What we now realize is they were simply studying us. They had been attracted to our world by the radio signals broadcast by our

Search for Extraterrestrial Intelligence program, and for the first few weeks after their landing they established communications with our computers. Quickly reassuring us that their intentions were not hostile, they began requesting digitized information about all earthly things. We were thrilled to oblige, and they consumed data at a prodigious rate. They easily learned several dozen human languages, and began communicating with reporters in their native tongues by means of linguistic conversion devices. Presently, they ventured out of the bays of their craft, their elephantine forms gliding with majestic dignity on furry pods, and, to the universal joy of the entire human race, the Intergalactic Epoch was born in that New Guinea field. All this is on film.

What is not on film is the expression on my face when the phone rang about a month later and a low-pitched metallic voice announced, "Mr. Gordon? This is Garto of Drune." The sound was obviously rendered by some sort of speech simulator, but I suspected something else. "Okay Eddie, stop screwing around. What do you want?"

"Who's that, dear?" My wife called from the kitchen.

"My brother, up to his usual unfunny pranks. He's talking into a cooking pot and expects me to believe it's the guy from outer space. Eddie, we're just sitting down to din . . ."

"This is Garto, Mr. Gordon. No joke."

"Tell him you'll call him back," my wife shouted. "The chicken will get cold."

"I'll get back to you, okay, *Garto*? Is there a number on the spaceship where I can reach you?"

"Now it's you who are joking," the voice said.

"Listen, chum, if you're Garto, send me a sign."

I had no sooner uttered the words than a shriek came from the kitchen and a horrible clatter of a metal tray crashing to the floor. I dropped the phone and rushed to the kitchen. On the floor was a live chicken flapping and squawking. Standing on the counter was my wife, also flapping and squawking.

Trembling, I picked up the extension in the kitchen. "Okay, Mister, you have my attention."

"I am Garto."

"I'll accept that as a working thesis."

"I wish to tell the story of my people, of our world, of my voyage."

"Could you talk a little louder? There's a woman screaming in here."

He repeated the message. "Now you definitely have my attention," I said. I put my finger over my lips and my wife, sensing that something extraordinary was happening, fell silent. "And how may I be of help to you?"

"I will need someone to represent me. You are universally admired, and from all we have been able to learn, you are an honest man. We have encountered very few here."

My wife implored me with her eyes to explain what was going on. I cupped my hand over the phone. "It's the guy from outer space. He wants me to be his agent."

"Sure," she said.

"If you need proof, I'll ask him to turn you into a chicken, too."

"No, thank you."

"What do I have to do?" I asked into the phone.

"Cancel your appointments and book a flight to New Guinea. I will contact you tomorrow to arrange details of our meeting."

"I will do so. But you owe me a chicken dinner for two."

As I hung up, the doorman buzzed us. My wife picked up the intercom. Her eyes widened.

"Who is it?" I asked.

"Maxie's Barbecue is on the way up," she said. "With chicken dinner for two."

And that is how I came to be the literary agent and personal manager of Garto and his contingent of Drunians. I will not go into the details of my trip to New Guinea and my personal experiences in getting to know the explorers from that distant world. Nor will I amplify on the way I created a business strategy for them, conducted their negotiations, and exploited their stories in every possible medium. It's fascinating, but not pertinent to this account. And besides, I've chronicled it in my memoir, *Agent to the Starfarers*. I cannot, however, resist the temptation to state that my clients made me a rich man, my agent colleagues became practically apoplectic with envy, and my wife treated me with a renewed respect bordering on reverence. I tried not to be insufferably smug with her, and succeeded most of the time.

When did it all go wrong, then? Well, whenever in the long sad chronicle of human history have things always gone wrong? When people get greedy, that's when. You would think that the countless publishers, movie studios, cable and television networks, media producers, product developers, commercial sponsors, and lawyers would have been content with the fortunes they made on the licenses I negotiated with them. But no, they couldn't let it go at that.

The big trouble began when Garto summoned me to Texas (where Disney had indeed established a theme park around the Drunian spacecraft). We hadn't talked face-to-face for six months; our frequent but routine conversations were usually conducted by telephone or televideo. Obviously, the matter he had to take up with me was far from routine: I could tell from the agitated timbre of his voice, even though communicated through his translation device. I caught the next plane to Houston.

I felt like a movie star on opening night as a guard ushered me up the spacecraft's ramp before the stares of thousands of fairground visitors. I found Garto in his chamber, the room redolent of his sweet-sour aroma to which I had never quite become accustomed. On the table before him were stacks of documents which I immediately recognized as book and movie contracts, as well as royalty statements issued by publishers, movie companies, and the countless merchandise firms that had licensed the rights to Drunian toys, games, clothes, furniture, tapes and records, and every other exploitable form of Druniana that the resourceful minds of businesspeople can conjure up.

"You have reviewed these?" he said without salutation.

"Of course."

"You know then that they are false."

I sat up sharply and paused to choose my reply carefully. "My accountants routinely audit them and have found no major discrepancies, Garto."

"They represent a fraction of what these works have actually earned. Where is the rest of our money?"

I picked a bunch of the papers up and examined them, finding nothing out of the ordinary.

"Perhaps you have misunderstood or misinterpreted the figures?"

He extended a pod and tapped a publisher's royalty statement. "Half of the money due on sales of this book are not reported."

I uttered a sigh of relief as I immediately saw what was troubling him. "I had told you at the outset that publishers sell books on consignment. They always hold back royalties to authors in case copies are returned."

"There are few returns of my books," Garto declared. I accepted this statement at face value. I had never doubted that Garto had ways of obtaining confidential information that was inaccessible to literary agents and other mere mortals.

"Perhaps your publishers have been overly zealous in withholding some of your money," I said. "Is something else bothering you?"

"They promised me an embossed foil cover. And my author's photo is blurry. But that is of no consequence compared to the missing royalties."

"No, I don't suppose it is. What else?"

He pushed another pile of papers at me. "Where are the rest of my movie profits?" he demanded.

"I told you about that, too, Garto, when you originally asked me to represent you."

"Remind me."

"Movie profits are calculated on a net basis, after deduction of certain defined expenses. The theater owners take a piece of every ticket sold at the box office, the distributor takes a bite, the movie studio writes off all sorts of deductible items and overhead . . ."

Garto cut me off with a majestic wave of his pod. "They are all lining their pockets every step of the way."

"That's showbiz," I quipped, hoping to lighten the atmosphere a bit, for the air was crackling with danger. "Seriously, Garto, movie studio accountants are among the most creative members of the human race. They have siphoned money from profit participants from the very beginning of the industry."

"That is neither an acceptable explanation nor a satisfactory excuse. I understand capitalism perfectly well and respect the desires of business firms to earn reasonable profits on their investments. The profits being earned by publishers, movie companies, and other licensees are flagrantly unreasonable, however. I want what is coming to me and my crewmates. And, by the way, they reneged on their promise of a full screen credit as technical consultant, and they never reimbursed my per diem expenses on location in Georgia."

"Rectifying that will be easier than making a studio cough up profits," I said. "You're looking at a long and honorable tradition of institutionalized fraud."

"If you cannot accomplish this, I will have to wonder whether, perhaps, even you are benefiting from these diversions of my funds."

I gasped. "My friend, I am appalled that you should even think such a thing."

"I want what is coming to me," he repeated.

"I will do what I can, Garto."

"You'll do more than that," he said. "And you'll do it within one week from this hour."

The latter was stated in a deadly flat tone that I had never heard in his voice before, but it chilled me to the marrow of my bones. So staggered was I by this ominous warning that it did not occur to me to ask what remedy he contemplated if I failed to carry out my mandate of redressing his grievance. For this oversight, it appears that the human race is about to pay dearly.

You will not be surprised to learn that I have spent the six and a half days and nights since that moment exerting the most determined effort in the history of the literary agents' profession to persuade publishers, movie executives, and merchandise manufacturers to refund the profits that Garto considered to be excessive. Most of you reading this narrative have the good fortune never to have encountered the mentality of accountants in the publishing and entertainment field, so you will simply have to take my word for it that my blandishments were greeted with derision to say the least. More common were the cynical jokes, at which I would have laughed had not the matter been as grave and desperate as it was. Indeed, in the good old, pre-Garto days, I had laughed at such jokes, and made up a few myself.

But I could not impress any of Garto's accounts payable that this was not merely a case of some naïve author bitching that the system was gypping him. My week of imploring, cajoling, and threatening yielded not a dime of reparations. One movie president summed up the prevailing attitude when he sneered, "Screw him! If he doesn't like the way we do business, he can zap us with his little ray gun."

Which brings us to what I believe to be the last moment of the human race. I calculate that we have about a half-hour. The Drunian craft hovers in the stratosphere, its "little ray gun" (or whatever weapon it employs) trained on our planet and its frail populace of fools and knaves. When it became clear, about an hour ago, that Garto had not been bluffing, I was inundated by panicky phone calls from many of Garto's debtors pressing settlements upon me. Their offers were in vain. Garto had stopped taking my phone calls.

As the clock moves inexorably toward doomsday, I am consumed by a single thought: Could Buddy Alter have structured Garto's deals better than I did?

■

Index

Books from Allworth Press

Mastering the Business of Writing: A Leading Literary Agent Reveals the Secrets of Success *by Richard Curtis* (softcover, 6 × 9, 272 pages, $18.95)

The Writer's and Photographer's Guide to Global Markets
by Michael Sedge (softcover, 6 × 9, 288 pages, $19.95)

How to Write Books that Sell, Second Edition
by L. Perry Wilbur and Jon Samsel (hardcover, 6 × 9, 224 pages, $19.95)

Writing for Interactive Media: The Complete Guide *by Jon Samsel and Darryl Wimberley* (hardcover, 6 × 9, 320 pages, $19.95)

The Writer's Internet Handbook *by Timothy K. Maloy*
(softcover, 6 × 9, 192 pages, $18.95)

The Writer's Legal Guide, Revised Edition
by Tad Crawford and Tony Lyons (softcover, 6 × 9, 304 pages, $19.95)

Business and Legal Forms for Writers and Self-Publishers, Revised Edition *by Tad Crawford* (softcover, 8½ × 11, 192 pages, $19.95)

The Writer's Resource Handbook *by Daniel Grant*
(softcover, 6 × 9, 272 pages, $19.95)

The Writer's Guide to Corporate Communications
by Mary Moreno (softcover, 6 × 9, 192 pages, $18.95)

Photography for Writers: Using Photography to Increase Your Writing Income *by Michael Havelin* (softcover, 6 × 9, 224 pages, $18.95)

Electronic Design and Publishing: Business Practices, Second Edition
by Liane Sebastian (softcover, 6¾ × 10, 216 pages, $19.95)

The Copyright Guide: A Friendly Guide for Protecting and Profiting from Copyrights *by Lee Wilson* (softcover, 6 × 9, 192 pages, $18.95)

Writing Scripts Hollywood Will Love: An Insider's Guide to Film and Television Scripts That Sell *by Katherine Atwell Herbert*
(softcover, 6 × 9, 160 pages, $12.95)

The Internet Research Guide *by Timothy K. Maloy*
(softcover, 6 × 9, 208 pages, $18.95)

Please write to request our free catalogue. To order by credit card, call 1-800-491-2808 or send a check or money order to Allworth Press, 10 East 23rd Street, Suite 210, New York, NY 10010. Include $5 for shipping and handling for the first book ordered and $1 for each additional book. Ten dollars plus $1 for each additional book if ordering from Canada. New York State residents must add sales tax.

If you would like to see our complete catalogue on the World Wide Web, you can find us at *www.allworth.com*